Casseroles

delicious one-pot wonders

THE AUSTRALIAN
Women's Weekly

contents

Casseroles feature in every clever cook's repertoire. They are fuss-free, flavoursome and always popular. Steaming one-pot wonders, these days, are brimming with many new flavour combinations, but traditional hearty fare is just as tempting. Some of our recipes for chicken, seafood and vegetarian are really quick, taking under 30 minutes to cook. To make this book even more helpful, there are ideas for cooking-ahead and freezing – a bonus when you're too busy to cook during the week. Before you start, read our casserole "basics" on page 4 for handy hints.

Pamela Clark
Food Director

tips for one-pot cooking

Follow this advice and make every casserole a fuss-free feast. From choosing the correct meat to preparation and cooking, these guidelines ensure the best results every time.

Casseroles are among the simplest of dishes. Once you've put the dish on to cook, your work is done – time and heat take care of the rest. It's the long, slow cooking that brings out the flavours and makes the meat succulent and tender. There are a few things you need to know, though, before you put your feet up.

choosing ingredients

Slow cooking in liquid tenderises even the toughest meat, so the cheaper cuts are suitable for casseroles. In fact, it's best to avoid the more expensive cuts, as they tend to be lean, and can become dry. Meat that is well marbled, or streaked with internal fat, is best; the fat melts after an hour or so in the dish, making the meat beautifully succulent. If you're making a beef casserole, look for chuck or round steak or gravy beef; if you're cooking lamb, buy chump chops or lamb shanks; if it's chicken, use drumsticks or thighs.

Root vegetables are the ones most often used in casseroles –

Marbled meat, perfect for casseroles

they're strongly flavoured and their starch content can help to thicken the sauce. Happily, they are usually the cheaper vegies. But don't make the mistake of buying vegetables past their prime; fresh is always best, even with long, slow cooking. Old vegies, as well as lacking nutrition, will not contribute much to the flavour of a casserole.

preparing the meat

Trim away any surplus fat from the meat first. The weights given in our recipes take this wastage into account. When cutting meat, cut across the grain. Conversely, when cutting a chicken thigh fillet, cut lengthways with the grain. This helps the chicken to keep its shape and produces a more tender dish.

flouring and browning

The first stage of the cooking process often involves coating the meat with flour and browning it in butter and/or oil. This process gives the meat a coating that seals in the flavour and juices. The flour also thickens the liquid during cooking, while browning imparts a good rich colour to the casserole.

Toss the meat in the flour just before browning. Don't do this ahead of time because the meat juices will absorb the flour and the coating will become gluey. You can put the meat in a bowl, turning the pieces in flour by hand, or throw everything in a clean plastic bag, toss it and shake off the excess flour.

Heat butter and/or oil in a heavy-base saucepan or flameproof casserole dish and add the floured meat, in batches. Sear the meat

Coating meat with flour in bowl

quickly over medium to high heat, turning the pieces until they are golden brown and sealed on all sides. Always be careful not to crowd the pan. If you try to cook too many pieces at once, they will stew rather than brown.

Browning meat in casserole dish

Adding stock to simmering casserole

cooking

Our recipes give you the approximate litre/cup capacity for cookware. The shape doesn't matter, however, if cookware is too small, food may boil over, and if too large, food may dry out. Flameproof dishes can be used in the oven as well as on the stove-top – these include cast-iron and stainless-steel dishes. Corningware and cast-iron dishes retain higher heat than most other cookware, so cooking time and temperature may need to be reduced slightly. To prevent sauce sticking, ensure the dish has a heavy base and a close-fitting lid, or is covered tightly with foil. Use a simmer mat on a gas burner, so the flame can be dispersed evenly and kept low.

As a rule, cooking time in the oven will be longer than on the stove-top. Simply continue to cook until meat is tender when pierced with a fork, or follow guidelines in the recipe. Many of these recipes can be adapted to cook in slow cookers or pressure cookers. Before you begin, read the manufacturer's instructions. Always follow all safety precautions.

The success of a casserole depends on long, slow simmering. Once the dish has been brought to a boil, reduce heat and simmer gently. If the liquid boils for an extended period, meat can become tough and dry.

make now, eat later

Casseroles are excellent do-ahead dishes. They don't suffer at all for being stored in the fridge for a day or two. In fact, many casseroles are much tastier after being left a while, as the flavours have had a chance to develop. You can also remove the fat when the casserole is cold, making it a much healthier dish.

Cook the casserole a day in advance and cool as quickly as possible. Hot food should be covered, then placed directly in the refrigerator to cool: modern refrigerators can cope with the load but you should place the hot dish on a heatproof tray at first to protect the shelf. Just before reheating, remove any fat that has solidified on top.

freezing

Unless they contain fish, dairy products, or are mainly made up of vegetables, casseroles can be frozen successfully. Cool the casserole in the refrigerator and remove and discard any fat. Spoon into a freezer container, leaving about 3cm at the top for expansion, or line a bowl with a plastic bag, spoon in the cooled casserole and freeze. Once the casserole is frozen, lift plastic bag out of the bowl and squeeze out any air, sealing with a tie. Casseroles can be frozen up to 2 months.

Thaw casserole in refrigerator overnight before reheating. Add green vegetables and dairy products just before serving. Also, check the consistency as flour-thickened sauces sometimes break down when frozen and you may need to re-thicken the casserole by adding a little extra blended flour and water, then stirring until mixture boils.

chicken

Take a tour around the kitchens of the world with these dishes which have chicken as their basis. Along with traditional favourites such as coq au vin and cacciatore we've included more recent additions such as a Moroccan-influenced tagine and Thai-style green curry.

spicy caribbean-style chicken stew

PREPARATION TIME 45 MINUTES • COOKING TIME 50 MINUTES

1kg chicken thigh fillets
2 teaspoons ground allspice
1 teaspoon ground cinnamon
pinch ground nutmeg
1 tablespoon finely chopped fresh thyme
1/4 cup (60ml) olive oil
2 medium brown onions (300g), sliced thinly
2 cloves garlic, crushed
1 tablespoon grated fresh ginger
1 teaspoon sambal oelek
5 medium tomatoes (650g), peeled, seeded, chopped finely
2 tablespoons brown sugar
2 teaspoons grated orange rind
2 tablespoons soy sauce
1 medium kumara (400g), chopped coarsely
2 fresh corn cobs, sliced thickly
125g baby spinach leaves

1 Cut chicken into 2cm strips. Toss chicken in combined spices and thyme.

2 Heat half of the oil in large saucepan; cook chicken, in batches, stirring, until browned. Drain on absorbent paper.

3 Heat remaining oil in pan. Cook onion, garlic, ginger and sambal oelek, stirring, until onion is soft.

4 Add tomato, sugar, rind, sauce, kumara, corn and chicken; cook, covered, about 15 minutes or until chicken and vegetables are tender. Remove cover; simmer 5 minutes.

5 Remove from heat. Add spinach; stir until spinach is wilted.

SERVES 6

per serving 22.3g fat; 1998kJ
store Recipe can be made a day ahead and refrigerated, covered. Recipe suitable to freeze.

coq au vin

PREPARATION TIME 20 MINUTES • COOKING TIME 1 HOUR

1.5kg chicken pieces
plain flour
40g butter
2 cloves garlic, crushed
3 bacon rashers (215g),
chopped finely
10 spring onions (250g), trimmed
200g swiss brown
mushrooms, halved
2 tablespoons brandy
1 cup (250ml) dry red wine
1 cup (250ml) chicken stock
1 sprig fresh parsley
2 teaspoons finely chopped
fresh thyme
1 bay leaf
2 tablespoons tomato paste

1 Toss chicken in flour; shake away excess flour. Heat butter in large saucepan; cook chicken until browned all over. Drain on absorbent paper.

2 Drain all but 1 tablespoon of the liquid from pan; cook garlic, bacon, onion and mushrooms, stirring, until onion is browned lightly.

3 Return chicken to pan. Add brandy, wine, stock, herbs, bay leaf and paste; simmer, covered, 30 minutes or until chicken is tender.

4 Remove chicken from pan; simmer sauce until thickened slightly. Discard bay leaf before serving.

5 Serve chicken with sauce.

SERVES 4

per serving 48.3g fat; 3170kJ
store Recipe can be made a day ahead and refrigerated, covered.

chicken marengo

PREPARATION TIME 20 MINUTES • COOKING TIME 1 HOUR 30 MINUTES

6 chicken thigh cutlets (1kg)
6 chicken drumsticks (900g)
2 tablespoons olive oil
250g button mushrooms
250g flat mushrooms, sliced thickly
2 medium brown onions
   (300g), sliced thickly
2 cloves garlic, crushed
2 tablespoons plain flour
1/2 cup (125ml) chicken stock
1/2 cup (125ml) dry white wine
1 tablespoon tomato paste
425g can tomatoes
1 tablespoon coarsely chopped
   fresh parsley

1 Remove skin from chicken.

2 Heat oil in 3.5 litre (14-cup) flameproof casserole dish; cook chicken, in batches, until browned. Drain on absorbent paper.

3 Drain all but 1 tablespoon of the liquid from dish; cook mushrooms, onion and garlic in dish, stirring, until onion is soft.

4 Add blended flour and stock, then wine, paste and undrained crushed tomatoes; stir over heat until mixture boils and thickens. Return chicken to dish; cook, covered, in moderate oven about 1 hour or until chicken is tender.

5 Serve sprinkled with parsley.

SERVES 6

per serving 21g fat; 1765kJ
store Recipe can be made a day ahead and refrigerated, covered.

chicken, date and honey tagine

PREPARATION TIME 20 MINUTES (plus refrigerating and standing time)
COOKING TIME 50 MINUTES

1 teaspoon salt
1 teaspoon cracked black pepper
1/2 teaspoon ground saffron
2 teaspoons ground cumin
8 chicken thigh cutlets (1.2kg)
30g butter
1 tablespoon olive oil
1 large brown onion (200g), chopped finely
1 cinnamon stick
11/2 cups (375ml) water
6 seedless fresh dates (150g)
2 teaspoons honey
1/4 cup (40g) blanched almonds, toasted

SAFFRON COUSCOUS
2 cups (500ml) chicken stock
pinch ground saffron
2 cups (300g) couscous
40g butter

1 Rub combined salt, pepper, saffron and cumin onto chicken. Cover; refrigerate 2 hours or overnight.

2 Heat butter and oil in large saucepan; cook chicken until browned. Remove from pan; drain all but 1 tablespoon of the liquid from pan. Add onion and cinnamon to pan; cook, stirring, until onion is soft.

3 Return chicken to pan. Add the water; simmer, covered, about 30 minutes or until chicken is tender. Add dates and honey; simmer, uncovered, 10 minutes or until thickened slightly.

4 Serve tagine with saffron couscous, sprinkled with nuts.

saffron couscous Boil stock in large saucepan with saffron. Remove from heat; stir in couscous. Stand 5 minutes; fluff using fork. Heat butter in pan. Add couscous; cook, stirring, until combined.

SERVES 4

per serving 40.8g fat; 3708kJ
store Recipe can be made a day ahead and refrigerated, covered. Tagine suitable to freeze; couscous not suitable.

chicken cacciatore

PREPARATION TIME 20 MINUTES • COOKING TIME 55 MINUTES

4 chicken marylands (1.4kg)
plain flour
1 tablespoon olive oil
2 cloves garlic, crushed
4 slices pancetta (60g),
  chopped coarsely
1 large brown onion (200g),
  chopped finely
1 medium (200g) yellow
  capsicum, chopped coarsely
3 medium tomatoes (450g),
  peeled, chopped coarsely
1/2 cup (125ml) dry white wine
1/2 cup (125ml) tomato puree
2 teaspoons finely chopped
  fresh sage
1 teaspoon finely chopped
  fresh rosemary
1 bay leaf

1 Cut chicken through joint into two pieces. Toss chicken in flour; shake away excess flour.

2 Heat oil in large saucepan; cook chicken, in batches, until browned all over. Drain on absorbent paper.

3 Drain all but 1 tablespoon of the juices from pan; cook garlic, pancetta, onion and capsicum, stirring, until onion is soft. Add tomato, wine and puree; simmer, uncovered, 2 minutes.

4 Return chicken to pan. Add herbs and bay leaf; simmer, covered, about 30 minutes or until chicken is tender. Discard bay leaf before serving.

SERVES 4

per serving 39.5g fat; 2636kJ
store Recipe can be made a day ahead and refrigerated, covered. Recipe suitable to freeze.

prosciutto-wrapped chicken

PREPARATION TIME 35 MINUTES • COOKING TIME 40 MINUTES

8 chicken thigh fillets (800g)
¹/₄ cup (20g) grated
  parmesan cheese
1 tablespoon coarsely chopped
  fresh oregano
4 small bocconcini cheese
  (200g), halved
8 slices prosciutto (120g)
2 tablespoons olive oil
1 clove garlic, crushed
6 medium tomatoes (780g),
  chopped coarsely
1 small brown onion (80g),
  chopped finely
¹/₄ cup (60ml) chicken stock
2 teaspoons balsamic vinegar
1 tablespoon coarsely chopped
  fresh parsley

1 Lightly pound fillets using meat mallet. Sprinkle each fillet with some of the combined parmesan cheese and oregano; top with bocconcini cheese. Roll up tightly; secure with toothpicks. Wrap prosciutto firmly around open ends of chicken to secure cheese.

2 Heat half of the oil in large saucepan; cook chicken, in batches, until browned all over. Remove from pan.

3 Heat remaining oil in pan; cook garlic, tomato and onion, stirring, about 5 minutes or until tomato and onion is soft.

4 Return chicken to pan. Add stock and vinegar; simmer, covered, 10 minutes.

5 Turn chicken; simmer, uncovered, about 10 minutes or until chicken is tender. Stir in parsley; remove and discard toothpicks.

6 Serve with pasta, if desired.

SERVES 4

per serving 34.8g fat; 2324kJ
store Recipe can be prepared a day ahead and refrigerated, covered. Recipe suitable to freeze.

african-style peanut, okra and tomato gumbo

PREPARATION TIME 30 MINUTES • COOKING TIME 50 MINUTES

300g okra
2 tablespoons peanut oil
800g chicken thigh fillets, chopped coarsely
2 large brown onions (400g), sliced thickly
3 cloves garlic, crushed
1 teaspoon sambal oelek
5 medium tomatoes (650g), peeled, seeded, chopped finely
1/4 cup (70g) tomato paste
1/3 cup (85g) crunchy peanut butter
1 large potato (300g), chopped coarsely
2 cups (500ml) water

1 Trim stems from okra. Heat half of the oil in large saucepan; cook chicken, in batches, stirring, until browned. Drain on absorbent paper.

2 Heat remaining oil in pan; cook onion, garlic and sambal oelek, stirring, until onion is soft.

3 Return chicken to pan. Add remaining ingredients; simmer, covered, about 30 minutes or until potato is tender.

SERVES 4

per serving 34.5g fat; 2517kJ
store Recipe best made just before serving.

chicken gumbo

PREPARATION TIME 30 MINUTES • COOKING TIME 1 HOUR 30 MINUTES

400g okra
12 chicken thigh cutlets (2kg)
2 tablespoons olive oil
2 medium brown onions (300g),
chopped finely
3 cloves garlic, crushed
1 medium green capsicum (200g),
chopped coarsely
1 medium red capsicum (200g),
chopped coarsely
1¹/₂ teaspoons cajun seasoning
¹/₂ teaspoon ground cumin
¹/₄ teaspoon cayenne pepper
2 bay leaves
2 cups (500ml) chicken stock
2 x 425g cans tomatoes
2 teaspoons worcestershire sauce

1 Trim stems from okra. Remove skin from chicken.

2 Heat oil in large saucepan; cook chicken, in batches, until browned all over. Drain on absorbent paper.

3 Add onion, garlic and okra to pan; cook, stirring, until onion is soft.

4 Return chicken to pan; cook capsicums, spices and bay leaves, stirring, until fragrant.

5 Add stock, undrained crushed tomatoes and sauce; simmer, covered, 1 hour.

6 Remove cover; simmer further 10 minutes or until thickened slightly. Discard bay leaves before serving.

SERVES 6

per serving 23.9g fat; 1924kJ
store Recipe can be made a day ahead and refrigerated, covered. Recipe suitable to freeze.

chilli tomato chicken

PREPARATION TIME 15 MINUTES • COOKING TIME 1 HOUR

12 chicken 'lovely legs' (1.5kg)
plain flour
2 tablespoons olive oil
1 medium red onion (150g),
  sliced thinly
2 cloves garlic, crushed
2 tablespoons pine nuts
2 small fresh red chillies,
  sliced thinly
3 bacon rashers, (220g)
  chopped coarsely
3 medium tomatoes (390g),
  peeled, chopped coarsely
1 cup (250ml) chicken stock
1/4 cup finely chopped
  fresh basil
1/4 cup (70g) tomato paste
1/2 cup (125ml) dry red wine
1/2 cup (80g) seeded
  black olives

1 Toss chicken in flour; shake away excess flour. Heat oil in large saucepan; cook chicken, in batches, until browned. Remove from pan.

2 Add onion, garlic, nuts, chilli and bacon to pan; cook, stirring, until onion is soft. Stir in tomato, stock, basil, paste, wine and olives.

3 Add chicken, simmer, uncovered, about 45 minutes or until chicken is tender.

SERVES 6

per serving 32.2g fat; 2134kJ
store Recipe can be made a day ahead and refrigerated, covered. Recipe suitable to freeze.

chicken, capsicum and caper stew

PREPARATION TIME 35 MINUTES • COOKING TIME 45 MINUTES

8 chicken drumsticks (1.2kg)
$^1/_4$ cup (35g) plain flour
1 teaspoon paprika
2 tablespoons olive oil
1 medium red capsicum (200g), chopped coarsely
1 medium yellow capsicum (200g), chopped coarsely
1 medium brown onion (150g), chopped coarsely
100g button mushrooms, halved
2 cloves garlic, crushed
1$^3/_4$ cups (430ml) chicken stock
$^1/_4$ cup (60ml) dry white wine
2 bay leaves
2 tablespoons drained tiny capers

1 Remove skin from chicken. Toss chicken in combined flour and paprika; shake away excess flour mixture.

2 Heat half of the oil in large saucepan; cook chicken, in batches, until browned all over. Remove from pan.

3 Heat remaining oil in pan; cook capsicums, onion, mushrooms and garlic, stirring, until onion is soft.

4 Return chicken to pan. Add stock, wine, bay leaves and capers; simmer, covered, 20 minutes, stirring occasionally.

5 Remove cover; simmer 10 minutes or until chicken is tender. Discard bay leaves before serving.

SERVES 4

per serving 21.9g fat; 1775kJ
store Recipe can be made a day ahead and refrigerated, covered. Recipe suitable to freeze.

green chicken curry with vegetables

PREPARATION TIME 35 MINUTES • COOKING TIME 50 MINUTES

1kg single chicken breast fillets
2 tablespoons peanut oil
1 large brown onion (200g),
   sliced thickly
1 medium green capsicum (200g),
   chopped coarsely
1 cup (250ml) chicken stock
280ml can coconut milk
1 dried lime leaf
360g baby bok choy,
   chopped coarsely
2 teaspoons cornflour
2 teaspoons water
¹/₄ cup finely shredded fresh basil

CURRY PASTE

1 small fresh green chilli
2 tablespoons finely chopped
   fresh lemon grass
1 tablespoon grated fresh ginger
2 cloves garlic, crushed

1 tablespoon fish sauce
1 tablespoon palm sugar
1 teaspoon ground coriander
¹/₂ teaspoon ground cumin
¹/₂ teaspoon ground ginger

1 Cut each fillet into three pieces. Heat half of the oil in large saucepan; cook chicken, in batches, until browned. Remove from pan.

2 Heat remaining oil in pan; cook onion, capsicum and curry paste, stirring, until onion is soft.

3 Return chicken to pan. Add stock, coconut milk and lime leaf; simmer, uncovered, about 20 minutes or until chicken is tender, stirring occasionally.

4 Add bok choy and blended cornflour and water; cook, stirring, until mixture boils and thickens slightly. Stir in basil. Discard lime leaf before serving.

curry paste Blend or process ingredients until combined.

SERVES 4

per serving 38.1g fat; 2652kJ
store Recipe best made just before serving.

moroccan-style chicken with almonds

PREPARATION TIME 30 MINUTES • COOKING TIME 40 MINUTES

**1 cup (170g) raisins,
    chopped coarsely
3 green onions, chopped finely
1 medium apple (150g),
    peeled, cored, grated
1 teaspoon ground ginger
1/2 cup (35g) stale breadcrumbs
14 chicken thigh fillets (1.5kg)
1 tablespoon olive oil
1/3 cup (55g) blanched
    almonds, toasted
1/2 cup (125ml) orange juice
1/4 cup (80g) plum jam
1/2 cup (125ml) dry white wine
1/2 teaspoon ground cinnamon
1 cup (250ml) chicken stock**

1 Combine raisins, onion, apple, ginger and breadcrumbs in large bowl; spread level tablespoons of mixture onto each thigh fillet. Roll up; secure with toothpicks.

2 Heat oil in large saucepan; cook chicken, in batches, until browned. Remove from pan.

3 Combine remaining ingredients in pan. Bring to a boil; return chicken to pan. Reduce heat; simmer, uncovered, about 20 minutes or until chicken is tender. Remove and discard toothpicks.

4 Serve sprinkled with extra toasted almonds and finely shredded green onions, if desired.

SERVES 6

per serving 26.9g fat; 2524kJ
store Recipe can be made a day ahead and refrigerated, covered. Recipe suitable to freeze.

chicken with lemon and rosemary

PREPARATION TIME 10 MINUTES • COOKING TIME 40 MINUTES

1 tablespoon olive oil
18 chicken thigh fillets (2kg)
3 cloves garlic, crushed
1 cup (250ml) chicken stock
$^1/_2$ cup (125ml) dry white wine
1 teaspoon grated lemon rind
2 tablespoons lemon juice
1 tablespoon coarsely chopped fresh rosemary
1 teaspoon cornflour
1 tablespoon water
$^1/_4$ cup (60ml) cream

1 Heat oil in large saucepan; cook chicken, in batches, until browned. Remove from pan.

2 Add garlic, stock, wine, rind, juice and rosemary to pan; bring to a boil.

3 Return chicken to pan. Reduce heat; simmer, uncovered, about 20 minutes or until chicken is tender. Remove chicken from pan.

4 Add blended cornflour and water to pan; stir over heat until sauce boils and thickens slightly. Reduce heat; add cream and chicken. Stir until hot.

5 Serve with green beans and new potatoes, if desired.

SERVES 6

per serving 31.6g fat; 2321kJ
store Recipe best made just before serving.
Recipe suitable to freeze.

chicken with red beans

PREPARATION TIME 15 MINUTES • COOKING TIME 35 MINUTES

1 tablespoon vegetable oil
1 medium brown onion (150g),
  chopped finely
2 medium red capsicums (400g),
  chopped finely
1 tablespoon drained, sliced
  canned jalapeno peppers
2 cloves garlic, crushed
1/2 teaspoon chilli powder
1 teaspoon paprika
1 teaspoon ground coriander
1 teaspoon ground cumin
750g minced chicken
2 x 310g cans red kidney beans,
  rinsed, drained
425g can tomatoes
2 tablespoons tomato paste
1 tablespoon finely chopped
  fresh parsley

1 Heat oil in large saucepan; cook onion, capsicum, pepper and garlic, stirring, until onion is soft.

2 Stir in chilli, paprika, coriander and cumin; cook, stirring, until fragrant.

3 Add chicken; cook, stirring, until browned.

4 Add beans, undrained crushed tomatoes, paste and parsley; cook, covered, about 15 minutes or until thickened slightly.

SERVES 6

per serving 14.1g fat; 1357kJ
store Recipe can be made a day ahead and refrigerated, covered. Recipe suitable to freeze.

hot and spicy chicken and kumara

PREPARATION TIME 30 MINUTES • COOKING TIME 1 HOUR

12 chicken thigh cutlets (2kg)
1/4 cup (35g) plain flour
2 teaspoons ground cumin
2 teaspoons paprika
2 teaspoons ground turmeric
2 tablespoons vegetable oil
1 medium brown onion
(150g), quartered
1 medium carrot (120g),
sliced thinly
2 cloves garlic, crushed
1 teaspoon sambal oelek
1 1/2 cups (375ml)
chicken stock
1/4 cup coarsely chopped
fresh coriander
1 medium kumara (400g),
chopped coarsely
1/4 cup (60ml) sour cream

1 Remove skin from chicken. Toss chicken in combined flour and spices; reserve remaining flour mixture.

2 Heat oil in large saucepan; cook chicken, in batches, until browned. Remove from pan.

3 Add onion, carrot, garlic and sambal oelek to pan; cook, stirring, until onion is soft. Add reserved flour mixture to pan; stir until mixture is dry and grainy.

4 Remove pan from heat; gradually stir in stock. Stir over heat until mixture boils and thickens slightly.

5 Return chicken to pan; simmer, uncovered, 20 minutes. Add coriander and kumara; simmer, uncovered, 15 minutes or until kumara is just tender. Stir in cream.

SERVES 6

per serving 27.6g fat; 2120kJ
store Recipe can be made a day ahead and refrigerated, covered; add sour cream after reheating. Recipe suitable to freeze.

herb-seasoned chicken with beer

PREPARATION TIME 25 MINUTES • COOKING TIME 40 MINUTES

8 chicken drumsticks (1.2kg)
plain flour
2 teaspoons vegetable oil
1 cup (250ml) beer
1/2 cup (125ml) chicken stock
1 tablespoon worcestershire sauce
2 teaspoons cornflour
2 teaspoons water

HERB SEASONING
2 bacon rashers (140g), chopped finely
3/4 cup (45g) stale breadcrumbs
40g butter, melted
1 tablespoon finely chopped fresh oregano
1 tablespoon finely chopped fresh chives
2 teaspoons finely chopped fresh thyme
1 teaspoon seasoned pepper

1 Push herb seasoning under skin of drumsticks; toss in flour. Shake away excess flour.

2 Heat oil in large saucepan; cook chicken, in batches, until browned.

3 Return chicken to pan. Add beer, stock and sauce; simmer, covered, about 20 minutes or until chicken is tender, stirring occasionally. Add blended cornflour and water; cook, stirring, until sauce boils and thickens.

4 Serve with pasta, if desired.

herb seasoning Heat large saucepan; cook bacon, stirring, until browned. Remove from heat; stir in remaining ingredients.

SERVES 4

per serving 31.5g fat; 2169kJ
store Seasoning can be made a day ahead; casserole can be made 3 hours ahead and refrigerated, covered.

indian-style curry with rice dumplings

PREPARATION TIME 40 MINUTES • COOKING TIME 1 HOUR

You will need to cook about 2/3 cup (130g) jasmine rice for this recipe.

1 tablespoon peanut oil
12 chicken thigh fillets
   (1.3kg), quartered
2 large brown onions (400g),
   sliced thinly
2 cloves garlic, crushed
2 teaspoons grated fresh ginger
1 teaspoon cumin seeds
1 teaspoon caraway seeds
2 tablespoons mild curry powder

425g can tomatoes
1/2 cup (125ml) chicken stock
1 tablespoon coarsely chopped
   fresh coriander

RICE DUMPLINGS
2 cups cooked jasmine rice
1 egg yolk
1 tablespoon finely chopped
   fresh coriander
1 cup (70g) stale breadcrumbs

1 Heat oil in large saucepan; cook chicken, in batches, stirring, until chicken is browned all over.

2 Return chicken to pan; cook onion, garlic, ginger, seeds and curry powder, stirring, until fragrant.

3 Add undrained crushed tomatoes and chicken stock; simmer, covered, 30 minutes.

4 Gently stir in rice dumplings; cook, uncovered, without boiling, until dumplings are just heated through. Serve sprinkled with coriander.

rice dumplings Process rice and egg yolk until rice is chopped and mixture combined; transfer rice mixture to large bowl. Add remaining ingredients; mix well. Using damp hands, roll level tablespoons of mixture into balls.

SERVES 6

per serving 21g fat; 1937kJ
store Curry and dumplings can be made a day ahead and refrigerated, covered separately.

Recipe suitable to freeze without dumplings.

curried lemon chicken

PREPARATION TIME 20 MINUTES • COOKING TIME 1 HOUR 20 MINUTES

12 chicken thigh cutlets (2kg)
plain flour
2 tablespoons vegetable oil
1 medium leek (350g),
** chopped coarsely**
2 trimmed sticks celery (150g),
** sliced thinly**
2 cloves garlic, crushed
2 teaspoons mild curry powder
1 tablespoon lemon juice
1 large green capsicum (350g),
** chopped finely**
250g button mushrooms
3 cups (750ml) chicken stock

1 Remove skin from chicken. Toss chicken in flour; shake away excess flour.

2 Heat oil in 3 litre (12-cup) flameproof casserole dish; cook chicken, in batches, until browned. Drain on absorbent paper.

3 Add leek, celery, garlic and curry powder to dish; cook, stirring, until leek is soft. Add juice, capsicum and mushrooms; cook, stirring, 2 minutes or until liquid evaporates.

4 Add chicken and stock; mix gently.

5 Cook, covered, in moderate oven about 1 hour or until chicken is tender.

SERVES 6

per serving 24g fat; 1862kJ

store Recipe can be made a day ahead and refrigerated, covered. Recipe suitable to freeze.

chicken cassoulet

PREPARATION TIME 25 MINUTES (plus standing time)
COOKING TIME 2 HOURS 30 MINUTES

1 cup (200g) dried haricot beans
500g spicy italian sausages
250g pork sausages
4 chicken thighs (900g)
4 single chicken breasts on the bone (1kg)
1 tablespoon vegetable oil
3 bacon rashers (215g), sliced thinly
2 cloves garlic, crushed
3 cloves
12 black peppercorns
1 trimmed stick celery (75g), cut into 5cm lengths
4 medium carrots (480g), sliced thinly
5 baby onions (125g), halved
$1/2$ cup (125ml) dry white wine
3 cups (750ml) water
2 tablespoons tomato paste

1 Place beans in large bowl; cover well with cold water. Cover; stand overnight.

2 Drain beans. Add sausages to large saucepan of boiling water. Boil, uncovered, 2 minutes; drain.

3 Remove skin from chicken; cut breasts in half.

4 Heat oil in 5 litre (20-cup) flameproof casserole dish; cook chicken and sausages, in batches, until browned. Drain on absorbent paper; slice sausages thickly.

5 Add bacon to dish; cook, stirring, until crisp. Drain on absorbent paper.

6 Return chicken to dish with beans, garlic, cloves, peppercorns, celery, carrot, onion, wine, the water and paste. Cook, covered, in moderate oven $1^1/_2$ hours.

7 Add sausages; cover. Cook about 30 minutes or until sausages are cooked. Serve sprinkled with bacon.

SERVES 8

per serving 42.1g fat; 2960kJ
store Recipe can be made a day ahead and refrigerated, covered. Recipe suitable to freeze.

chicken sausages with beans

PREPARATION TIME 15 MINUTES • COOKING TIME 45 MINUTES

2 medium red capsicums (400g)
1 tablespoon vegetable oil
800g chicken sausages
2 medium brown onions (300g),
**   sliced thinly**
3 cloves garlic, crushed
4 bacon rashers (285g),
**   chopped finely**
440g can baked beans in
**   tomato sauce**
425g can tomatoes
¹/₄ cup (60ml)
**   worcestershire sauce**
2 tablespoons coarsely chopped
**   fresh parsley**

1 Quarter capsicums; remove seeds and membranes. Grill capsicum, skin side up, until skin blisters and blackens. Peel away skin; chop capsicum.

2 Heat oil in large saucepan; cook sausages until browned. Remove from pan; cut sausages in half.

3 Add onion to pan with garlic and bacon; cook, stirring, until onion is soft and bacon is browned lightly.

4 Add beans, undrained crushed tomatoes, sauce, capsicum and sausage; simmer, covered, 20 minutes.

5 Serve sprinkled with parsley.

SERVES 6

per serving 36.1g fat; 2134kJ

store Recipe can be made a day ahead and refrigerated, covered. Recipe suitable to freeze.

chicken with mushrooms and celeriac

PREPARATION TIME 35 MINUTES • COOKING TIME 1 HOUR 30 MINUTES

2 large red capsicums (700g)
8 chicken thigh cutlets (1.2kg)
plain flour
1 tablespoon olive oil
1¹/₂ teaspoons caraway seeds
5 dried juniper berries
1 medium celeriac (630g),
  chopped coarsely
250g button mushrooms, halved
1¹/₂ cups (375ml) chicken stock
1 tablespoon tomato paste
3 teaspoons cornflour
1 tablespoon water
1 tablespoon finely chopped
  fresh parsley

1 Quarter capsicums; remove seeds and membranes. Grill capsicum, skin side up, until skin blisters and blackens. Peel away skin; slice capsicum into strips.

2 Toss chicken in flour; shake away excess flour. Heat oil in 3 litre (12-cup) flameproof casserole dish; cook chicken, in batches, until browned. Drain on absorbent paper.

3 Add seeds, berries, celeriac and mushrooms to dish; cook, stirring, until mushrooms are just soft.

4 Return chicken to dish with capsicum, stock and paste; mix well. Cook, covered, in moderate oven about 45 minutes or until chicken is tender.

5 Stir in blended cornflour and water. Stir over heat until mixture boils and thickens slightly.

6 Serve sprinkled with parsley.

SERVES 4

per serving 32.4g fat; 2187kJ
store Recipe can be made a day ahead and refrigerated, covered. Recipe suitable to freeze.

beef

Bring out the best in beef with these recipes ranging from hearty family favourites such as steak and kidney pie and oxtail stew to more exotic offerings such as chilli marinated beef in coconut curry sauce.

chilli con carne

PREPARATION TIME 25 MINUTES • COOKING TIME 1 HOUR 30 MINUTES

1kg beef chuck steak
2 tablespoons olive oil
2 medium brown onions (300g), chopped finely
3 cloves garlic, crushed
3 teaspoons ground cumin
1 teaspoon ground coriander
1 teaspoon chilli powder
1 tablespoon finely chopped fresh oregano
2 x 425g cans tomatoes
1 cup (250ml) beef stock
2 teaspoons brown sugar
310g can red kidney beans, rinsed, drained

1 Cut beef into 2cm pieces. Heat half of the oil in large saucepan; cook beef, in batches, until browned. Drain on absorbent paper.

2 Heat remaining oil in pan; cook onion, garlic, spices and oregano, stirring, until onion is soft.

3 Add undrained crushed tomatoes, stock, sugar and beef; simmer, covered, about 1 hour or until beef is tender.

4 Stir beans into beef mixture; simmer 5 minutes or until heated through.

SERVES 6

per serving 14.9g fat; 1484kJ
store Recipe can be made a day ahead and refrigerated, covered. Recipe suitable to freeze.

beef and vegetables with beer

PREPARATION TIME 15 MINUTES • COOKING TIME 1 HOUR 45 MINUTES

1¹/₂ tablespoons vegetable oil
1.5kg rolled roast of beef brisket
2 large carrots (360g),
**   chopped coarsely**
2 large parsnips (360g),
**   chopped coarsely**
6 baby onions (150g)
6 baby new potatoes (240g)
2 x 375ml cans beer

1 Heat oil in large baking dish;
  cook beef until browned. Remove
  from dish.

2 Add vegetables to dish; cook,
  stirring, until browned all over.

3 Return beef to dish; add beer.
  Cook, covered, in moderately hot
  oven 45 minutes.

4 Remove vegetables to flat oven
  tray. Cover loosely with foil;
  return to oven.

5 Turn beef; cook, uncovered,
  about 30 minutes or until beef
  is cooked through. Remove beef
  from dish; wrap in foil.

6 Place baking dish over heat;
  simmer, uncovered, until liquid
  reduces to about 1 cup (250ml).

7 Serve sliced beef with vegetables
  and sauce.

SERVES 6

per serving 16.6g fat; 2016kJ
store Recipe best made just
before serving.

steak and kidney pie

PREPARATION TIME 25 MINUTES • COOKING TIME 1 HOUR 30 MINUTES

300g beef ox kidneys
1.5g beef chuck steak,
  chopped coarsely
2 medium brown onions
  (300g), sliced thinly
1 cup (250ml) beef stock
1 tablespoon soy sauce
1/4 cup (35g) plain flour
1/2 cup (125ml) water
2 sheets ready-rolled
  puff pastry
1 egg, beaten lightly

1 Remove fat from kidneys; chop
   kidneys finely. Combine kidneys,
   beef, onion, stock and sauce in
   large saucepan; simmer, covered,
   about 1 hour or until beef is
   tender.

2 Stir blended flour and water into
   beef mixture; stir until mixture
   boils and thickens. Transfer to
   1.5 litre (6-cup) ovenproof dish.

3 Cut pastry into 6cm rounds.
   Overlap rounds on beef mixture;
   brush with egg. Cook in
   moderate oven about
   15 minutes or until browned.

SERVES 6

per serving 26.7g fat; 2598kJ
store Recipe can be
prepared a day ahead and
refrigerated, covered.
Beef mixture suitable to freeze.

beef and three potato hot pot

PREPARATION TIME 30 MINUTES • COOKING TIME 2 HOURS 30 MINUTES

2kg beef chuck steak, chopped coarsely
plain flour
1/4 cup (60ml) vegetable oil
2 large brown onions (400g), chopped finely
4 bacon rashers (285g), chopped coarsely
1 litre (4 cups) beef stock
1 small kumara (250g), chopped coarsely
4 baby new potatoes (160g)
200g white sweet potato, chopped coarsely
2 tablespoons coarsely chopped fresh thyme
1 tablespoon tomato paste
1 tablespoon finely chopped fresh parsley

1 Toss beef in flour; shake away excess flour. Heat half of the oil in 2.5 litre (10-cup) flameproof casserole dish; cook onion and bacon, stirring, until onion is soft. Remove from dish.

2 Heat remaining oil in dish; cook beef, in batches, until browned.

3 Return onion mixture to dish; stir in stock. Cook, covered, in moderate oven 1 hour.

4 Add kumara, potatoes and thyme. Cook, covered, 1 hour or until beef is tender.

5 Stir in paste; serve sprinkled with parsley.

SERVES 8

per serving 20.5g fat; 2064kJ
store Recipe can be made a day ahead and refrigerated, covered. Recipe suitable to freeze.

chilli beef and beans

PREPARATION TIME 15 MINUTES • COOKING TIME 2 HOURS 20 MINUTES

1.5kg beef chuck steak
1 tablespoon vegetable oil
1 large brown onion
   (200g), chopped
3 cloves garlic, crushed
1 teaspoon ground cumin
1 teaspoon chilli powder
1 medium green capsicum
   (200g), chopped
2 x 310g cans red kidney beans,
rinsed, drained
425g can tomato puree
425g can tomatoes,
   undrained, crushed
1 teaspoon dried oregano
1/4 cup (60ml) corn relish
1 beef stock cube
1 teaspoon sugar

1 Preheat oven to moderately slow.
   Cut beef into 3cm pieces.

2 Heat oil in flameproof 2.5-litre
   (10 cup) casserole dish; cook
   beef, in batches, stirring, until
   browned. Remove from dish.

3 Add onion, garlic and spices
   to same dish; cook, stirring,
   until onion is soft. Return
   beef to dish with remaining
   ingredients; bring to a boil.

4 Transfer dish to oven; bake,
   covered, in moderately slow oven
   about 2 hours or until
   beef is tender.

SERVES 6

per serving 15.3g fat; 1912kJ
store Recipe can be made a day
ahead and refrigerated, covered.
Recipe suitable to freeze.

beef bourguignon

PREPARATION TIME 25 MINUTES • COOKING TIME 2 HOURS 30 MINUTES

1kg beef chuck steak
2 tablespoons vegetable oil
60g butter
10 baby onions (250g)
400g button mushrooms
3 bacon rashers (210g),
chopped coarsely
1 clove garlic, crushed
¼ cup (35g) plain flour
1 cup (250ml) beef stock
1 cup (250ml) dry red wine
2 bay leaves
1 tablespoon brown sugar
3 teaspoons finely chopped
fresh oregano

1 Cut beef into 3cm pieces. Heat half of the oil in large saucepan; cook beef, in batches, until browned. Remove from pan.

2 Heat remaining oil and butter in pan; cook onions, mushrooms, bacon and garlic, stirring, until onions are browned lightly. Stir in flour; stir over heat until mixture is browned.

3 Remove from heat. Gradually stir in stock and wine; stir over heat until sauce boils and thickens.

4 Return beef and any juices to pan; add bay leaves, sugar and oregano. Simmer, covered, about 2 hours or until beef is tender, stirring occasionally. Discard bay leaves.

SERVES 4

per serving 36.3g fat; 2890kJ
store Recipe can be made a day ahead and refrigerated, covered. Recipe suitable to freeze.

family beef casserole

PREPARATION TIME 15 MINUTES • COOKING TIME 2 HOURS 15 MINUTES

2 tablespoons vegetable oil
2kg beef chuck steak, chopped coarsely
2 medium brown onions (300g), sliced thinly
2 medium carrots (240g), sliced thickly
3 cloves garlic, crushed
1/4 cup finely chopped fresh parsley
1/4 cup (70g) tomato paste
2 teaspoons french mustard
1 cup (250ml) dry red wine
1/2 cup (125ml) beef stock

1 Heat oil in 2.5 litre (10-cup) flameproof casserole dish; cook beef, in batches, until browned. Remove from dish.

2 Add onion, carrot and garlic to dish; cook, stirring, until onion is soft.

3 Return beef to dish; stir in parsley, paste, mustard, wine and stock. Cook, covered, in slow oven about 1³/4 hours or until beef is tender.

SERVES 6

per serving 23g fat; 2318kJ
store Recipe can be prepared a day ahead and refrigerated, covered. Recipe suitable to freeze.

oxtail stew

PREPARATION TIME 25 MINUTES • COOKING TIME 2 HOURS

2kg coarsely chopped oxtail
plain flour
60g ghee
2 large brown onions (400g),
 sliced thinly
2 cloves garlic, crushed
2 teaspoons coarsely chopped
 fresh rosemary
1/4 cup (60ml) dry red wine
2 large parsnips (360g),
 sliced thickly
2 medium carrots (240g),
 sliced thickly
3 cups (750ml) beef stock
1 teaspoon freshly ground
 black pepper
2 medium zucchini (240g),
 sliced thickly
1 cup (250ml) tomato puree
1 tablespoon coarsely chopped
 fresh parsley

1 Toss oxtail in flour; shake away excess flour. Heat ghee in large saucepan; cook oxtail, in batches, stirring, until browned well all over. Drain on absorbent paper.

2 Add onion, garlic and rosemary to pan; cook, stirring, until onion is soft.

3 Add wine; cook, stirring, until liquid reduces by a half.

4 Return oxtail to pan; add parsnip, carrot, stock and pepper. Cook, covered, 1 1/4 hours.

5 Add zucchini, puree and parsley; cook, uncovered, 20 minutes or until oxtail is tender.

SERVES 6

per serving 68.8g fat; 3664kJ
store Recipe best made a day ahead and refrigerated, covered. Recipe suitable to freeze.

spare ribs in oregano mushroom sauce

PREPARATION TIME 15 MINUTES • COOKING TIME 2 HOURS 15 MINUTES

1.5kg beef spare ribs
plain flour
1/4 cup (60ml) olive oil
1 clove garlic, crushed
1 tablespoon finely chopped fresh oregano
2 large brown onions (400g), sliced thinly
3 medium potatoes (600g), chopped coarsely
250g button mushrooms
3 cups (750ml) beef stock
20 baby carrots
2 tablespoons tomato paste

1 Toss ribs in flour; shake away excess flour. Heat 2 tablespoons of the oil in large saucepan; cook ribs, in batches, until browned all over. Drain on absorbent paper.

2 Heat remaining oil in pan; cook garlic, oregano and onion, stirring, until onion is soft. Add potato, mushrooms and stock.

3 Return ribs to pan; cook, covered, 1 1/4 hours.

4 Add carrots and paste; cook, uncovered, about 10 minutes or until carrots are tender.

SERVES 6

per serving 21.4g fat; 2029kJ
store Recipe can be made a day ahead and refrigerated, covered. Recipe suitable to freeze.

country-style beef and mushrooms

PREPARATION TIME 30 MINUTES • COOKING TIME 1 HOUR 30 MINUTES

2 large red capsicums (700g)
2 tablespoons olive oil
1.5kg beef blade steak, chopped coarsely
20g butter
2 cloves garlic, crushed
1 medium fennel bulb (620g), cut into wedges
200g button mushrooms
200g swiss brown mushrooms, halved
200g shiitake mushrooms, quartered
2 cups (500ml) beef stock
$1/2$ cup (100g) barley
500g english spinach, shredded thickly

1 Quarter capsicums; remove seeds and membranes. Grill capsicum, skin side up, until skin blisters and blackens. Peel away skin; cut capsicum into thick strips.

2 Heat half of the oil in large saucepan; cook beef, in batches, stirring, until browned. Remove from pan.

3 Heat remaining oil and butter in pan; cook garlic, fennel and mushrooms, stirring, until fennel is tender.

4 Return beef to pan; add capsicum, stock and barley. Simmer, covered, about 1 hour or until beef is tender.

5 Add spinach; stir until just wilted.

SERVES 6

per serving 21.9g fat; 2227kJ
store Recipe can be prepared a day ahead and refrigerated, covered; add spinach just before serving.
Beef mixture suitable to freeze; add spinach just before serving.

48

beef diane

PREPARATION TIME 20 MINUTES • COOKING TIME 2 HOURS

1kg beef chuck steak
1 tablespoon olive oil
4 cloves garlic, crushed
1 medium brown onion (150g), chopped finely
425g can tomatoes
1/2 cup (125ml) beef stock
2 tablespoons worcestershire sauce
1/2 cup (125ml) cream
2 tablespoons coarsely chopped fresh parsley
1 tablespoon brandy

1 Cut beef into 3cm pieces. Heat oil in large saucepan; cook beef, in batches, stirring, until browned.

2 Add garlic and onion; cook, stirring, until onion is soft.

3 Add undrained crushed tomatoes, stock and sauce; simmer, covered, about 1½ hours or until beef is tender.

4 Add remaining ingredients; simmer, uncovered, about 5 minutes or until thickened slightly.

5 Serve with pasta and sprinkled with extra chopped parsley, if desired.

SERVES 4

per serving 30.5g fat; 2255kJ
store Recipe can be made a day ahead and refrigerated, covered.
Recipe suitable to freeze; stir in cream, parsley and brandy just before serving.

fruity beef and eggplant tagine

PREPARATION TIME 45 MINUTES (plus standing time) • COOKING TIME 2 HOURS

1 medium eggplant (300g)
coarse cooking salt
1 tablespoon olive oil
1/2 teaspoon ground cinnamon
1/4 teaspoon ground turmeric
1/2 teaspoon ground ginger
1/4 teaspoon ground cumin
1/4 teaspoon ground coriander
1kg beef chuck steak,
**   chopped coarsely**
1 medium brown onion
**   (150g), grated**
2 cloves garlic, crushed
425g can tomatoes, drained
3 cups (750ml) beef stock
2 strips lemon rind
1 cinnamon stick
1 cup (170g) seeded prunes
2 tablespoons finely chopped
**   fresh coriander**
1 tablespoon sesame
**   seeds, toasted**

1 Cut eggplant into 1cm slices; place slices in colander. Sprinkle with salt; stand 30 minutes. Rinse slices under cold water; drain on absorbent paper. Cut eggplant slices into quarters.

2 Heat oil in large saucepan; cook ground spices and beef, stirring, until browned. Add onion and garlic; cook, stirring, 5 minutes.

3 Stir in crushed tomatoes, stock, rind and cinnamon; simmer, covered, about 1 hour or until beef is tender.

4 Add eggplant and prunes; simmer, uncovered, 30 minutes. Discard rind and cinnamon stick; stir in half of the fresh coriander.

5 Serve sprinkled with remaining fresh coriander and sesame seeds.

6 Serve with couscous if desired.

SERVES 4

per serving 19.3g fat; 2179kJ
store Recipe can be made a day ahead and refrigerated, covered.
Recipe suitable to freeze.

chilli marinated beef in coconut curry sauce

PREPARATION TIME 20 MINUTES (plus marinating time) • COOKING TIME 2 HOURS

1.5kg beef chuck steak, chopped coarsely
40g ghee
2 medium red capsicums (400g), chopped finely
2 medium brown onions (300g), chopped finely
1/2 cup (125ml) beef stock
1/2 cup (125ml) coconut milk
1 cinnamon stick
5 dried curry leaves
1 tablespoon finely chopped fresh coriander

MARINADE
1/3 cup (80ml) white vinegar
2 small fresh red chillies, sliced thinly
2 tablespoons tomato paste
1 tablespoon finely chopped fresh coriander
2 cloves garlic, crushed
3 cardamom pods, crushed
2 teaspoons cumin seeds
1 teaspoon ground turmeric

1 Combine beef and marinade in large bowl; mix well. Cover; refrigerate several hours or overnight.

2 Heat half of the ghee in large saucepan; cook beef, in batches, stirring, until browned. Remove from pan.

3 Heat remaining ghee in same pan; cook capsicum and onion, stirring, until onion is soft.

4 Return beef to pan; add stock, coconut milk, cinnamon and curry leaves. Simmer, covered, 1 hour, stirring occasionally.

5 Remove cover; simmer about 30 minutes or until beef is tender. Discard cinnamon stick; stir in coriander.

6 Serve with steamed or boiled rice, if desired.

marinade Combine ingredients in large bowl; mix well.

SERVES 6

per serving 23.2g fat; 1929kJ
store Recipe can be made a day ahead and refrigerated, covered. Recipe suitable to freeze.

beef in red wine sauce with roasted tomatoes

PREPARATION TIME 20 MINUTES • COOKING TIME 2 HOURS 30 MINUTES

8 medium egg tomatoes
  (600g), halved
1/4 cup (60ml) olive oil
2 cloves garlic, crushed
1 teaspoon brown sugar
4 bacon rashers (285g),
  sliced thinly
1 medium carrot (120g),
  sliced thinly
1 medium brown onion
  (150g), chopped coarsely
12 baby onions (300g)
250g button mushrooms
1.5kg beef chuck steak,
  chopped coarsely
2 tablespoons plain flour
3 cups (750ml) dry red wine
1 bay leaf
2 tablespoons cornflour
1 cup (250ml) water
2 tablespoons chopped
  fresh parsley

1 Place tomato, cut side up, on oven tray. Combine 1 tablespoon of the oil with garlic in small bowl. Brush tomato with oil mixture; sprinkle with sugar. Bake, uncovered, in moderate oven about 30 minutes or until tomato is tender.

2 Heat 1 tablespoon of the remaining oil in 3 litre (12-cup) flameproof casserole dish; cook bacon, stirring, until browned lightly. Drain on absorbent paper.

3 Add carrot and brown onion to dish. Cook, stirring, until browned lightly; remove from dish. Add baby onions and mushrooms to dish. Cook, stirring, until onions are browned lightly; remove from dish.

4 Heat remaining oil in dish; cook beef, in batches, stirring, until browned. Add flour; cook, stirring, 2 minutes. Add wine, bacon, brown onion mixture and bay leaf to dish; cook, covered, in moderate oven about 1 hour.

5 Stir in mushrooms and baby onions, then blended cornflour and water. Cook, covered, about 45 minutes or until beef is tender. Discard bay leaf; gently stir in tomato and parsley.

SERVES 8

per serving 17.6g fat; 1894kJ
store Recipe can be made a day ahead and refrigerated, covered. Recipe suitable to freeze; stir in tomato and parsley after reheating.

prosciutto and beef roll

PREPARATION TIME 30 MINUTES • COOKING TIME 3 HOURS 30 MINUTES

1.7kg piece of beef chuck steak
4 slices prosciutto (60g)
2 tablespoons olive oil
10 baby onions (250g)
12 baby new potatoes (480g)
1 cup (250ml) dry red wine
1/2 cup (125ml) beef stock
425g can tomatoes, drained,
chopped finely
1 sprig fresh thyme
1 sprig fresh parsley
1 sprig fresh rosemary
2 fresh sage leaves
1 tablespoon cornflour
1 tablespoon water

1 Place beef, cut side up, on board; top with prosciutto. Roll up firmly; secure with string at 2cm intervals.

2 Heat oil in baking dish; cook beef until browned all over. Remove from dish.

3 Add onions and potatoes to dish; cook, stirring, until browned lightly.

4 Return beef to dish; add wine, stock and tomato.

5 Place herbs in a piece of muslin; tie securely with string. Add herbs to dish; cook, covered, in slow oven about 3 hours or until beef is tender. Baste several times during cooking.

6 Remove beef and vegetables from dish; add blended cornflour and water to pan juices. Stir over heat until mixture boils and thickens; discard herbs.

7 Serve sliced beef with vegetables and sauce.

SERVES 8

per serving 15.2g fat; 1693kJ
store Recipe can be prepared a day ahead and refrigerated, covered.
Recipe suitable to freeze; thicken with cornflour just before serving.

purees and mashes

basic mashed potato

PREPARATION TIME 15 MINUTES • COOKING TIME 20 MINUTES

4 medium old potatoes (800g)
40g butter
1/4 cup (60ml) milk
1 teaspoon brown sugar

1   Peel potatoes; cut each into four even pieces. Boil, steam or microwave potatoes until tender; drain. Mash well using potato masher or fork, or push potato through sieve.

2   Add butter, milk and sugar, beat until butter melts.

SERVES 4

per serving 9g fat; 911kJ

store Recipe and variations best made just before serving.

mashed potato variations

LEEK AND THYME

PREPARATION TIME 20 MINUTES
COOKING TIME 25 MINUTES

1 tablespoon vegetable oil
1 small leek (200g), sliced thinly
1 clove garlic, crushed
1 tablespoon finely chopped
**   fresh thyme**
2 tablespoons dry white wine

Heat oil in large saucepan; cook leek, garlic and thyme, stirring, until leek is soft. Add wine; cook, stirring, until wine evaporates. Stir leek mixture into basic mashed potato.

SERVES 4

per serving 13.7g fat; 1144kJ

ITALIAN

PREPARATION TIME 20 MINUTES
COOKING TIME 20 MINUTES

1/4 cup (20g) grated
**   parmesan cheese**
1/4 cup (40g) sliced seeded
**   black olives**
1 tablespoon finely chopped
**   fresh basil**

Add cheese, olives and basil to mashed potato; mix well

SERVES 4

per serving 10.7g fat; 1046kJ

PINE NUT

PREPARATION TIME 15 MINUTES
COOKING TIME 25 MINUTES

1/3 cup (50g) pine nuts, toasted
2 teaspoons finely chopped
**   fresh rosemary**

Add pine nuts and rosemary to basic mashed potato; mix well.

SERVES 4

per serving 17.8g fat; 1271k

BACON AND MUSTARD

PREPARATION TIME 20 MINUTES
COOKING TIME 25 MINUTES

4 bacon rashers (285g),
**   chopped finely**
3 teaspoons seeded mustard
1 tablespoon finely chopped
**   fresh parsley**

Cook bacon in large frying pan until crisp; drain on absorbent paper. Add bacon, mustard and parsley to basic mashed potato; mix well.

SERVES 4

per serving 12.3g fat; 1170kJ

THAI-STYLE

PREPARATION TIME 20 MINUTES
COOKING TIME 25 MINUTES

1/4 cup (60ml) coconut cream
1 tablespoon vegetable oil
1 small brown onion (80g),
**   chopped finely**
1 clove garlic, crushed
1 small fresh red chilli, seeded,
**   chopped finely**
1 teaspoon grated fresh ginger
1 tablespoon finely chopped
**   fresh coriander**

Substitute coconut cream for milk in basic mashed potato recipe. Heat oil in large saucepan; cook onion, garlic, chilli and ginger, stirring, until onion is soft. Add to mashed potato with coriander; mix well.

SERVES 4

per serving 16.8g fat; 1241kJ

CAJUN

PREPARATION TIME 25 MINUTES
COOKING TIME 30 MINUTES

**1 small red capsicum (150g),
  roasted, sliced thinly**
1/2 teaspoon cajun seasoning
**1 teaspoon finely chopped
  fresh thyme**

Add capsicum, spice mix and thyme
to basic mashed potato; mix well.

SERVES 4

per serving 9.1g fat; 947kJ

parsnip puree

PREPARATION TIME 15 MINUTES
COOKING TIME 20 MINUTES

**6 large parsnips (1kg),
  chopped finely**
1 teaspoon seasoned pepper
40g butter
2 tablespoons cream
**1 tablespoon finely chopped
  fresh parsley**

Boil, steam or microwave parsnips
until tender; drain. Blend or
process parsnips with remaining
ingredients until smooth.

SERVES 6

per serving 3.8g fat; 482kJ

creamy roasted kumara puree

PREPARATION TIME 15 MINUTES
COOKING TIME 50 MINUTES

1 large kumara (550g)
**2/3 cup (160ml)
  thickened cream**
1/4 teaspoon ground cumin
1/4 teaspoon mixed spice

1 Cut kumara into 4cm chunks;
  place onto oven tray. Cover; bake
  in moderately hot oven about 50
  minutes or until tender.

2 Blend or process kumara
  with remaining ingredients
  until smooth.

SERVES 4

per serving 15g fat; 963kJ

lamb

Lamb lends itself to gentle cooking, enhancing the meat's succulence and sweetness. This collection of recipes includes updated classics such as pot roasts, braises and stews as well as Mediterranean-influenced offerings including lamb with Madeira and olive sauce.

lamb with rosemary and vegetables

PREPARATION TIME 30 MINUTES • COOKING TIME 1 HOUR 20 MINUTES

1.5kg lamb neck chops
1 tablespoon vegetable oil
2 cloves garlic, crushed
2 medium leeks (700g), chopped finely
8 baby onions (200g), halved
2 medium parsnips (250g), chopped coarsely
1 medium kumara (400g), chopped coarsely
1 cup (250ml) dry red wine
1 cup (250ml) beef stock
1/3 cup (95g) tomato paste
400g can tomatoes
2 medium zucchini (240g), chopped coarsely
2 teaspoons finely chopped fresh rosemary

1 Trim fat from chops. Heat oil in large saucepan; cook chops until well browned.

2 Add garlic, leek, onion, parsnip, kumara, wine, stock, paste and undrained crushed tomatoes; simmer, covered, 1 hour, stirring occasionally.

3 Stir in zucchini and rosemary; simmer, covered, 10 minutes or until chops are tender.

SERVES 4

per serving 17.4g fat; 2022kJ
store Recipe can be made a day ahead and refrigerated, covered. Recipe suitable to freeze.

58

garlic and rosemary lamb pot roast

PREPARATION TIME 20 MINUTES • COOKING TIME 3 HOURS

2 x 900g boned rolled lamb shoulders
4 cloves garlic, halved
4 small sprigs fresh rosemary
2 tablespoons olive oil
10 baby onions (250g)
12 baby new potatoes (480g)
10 baby carrots
1/2 cup (125ml) chicken stock
1 cup (250ml) dry white wine
3 finger eggplants (180g), sliced thickly
425g can tomatoes
2 tablespoons sour cream

1 Using the point of a small knife, cut small slits in lamb and insert garlic pieces and tiny sprigs of rosemary.

2 Heat oil in 4 litre (16-cup) flameproof casserole dish; cook lamb until browned all over.

3 Add onions, potatoes, carrots, stock and wine; cook, covered, in moderately slow oven 2 hours.

4 Add eggplant and undrained crushed tomatoes; cook, uncovered, about 30 minutes or until lamb is tender.

5 Remove lamb and vegetables from dish; keep warm. Bring pan juices to a boil; reduce heat. Simmer, uncovered, until reduced to about 1¹/₂ cups (375ml); stir in sour cream.

6 Serve sliced lamb with vegetables and sauce.

SERVES 8

per serving 19.7g fat; 1875kJ
store Recipe best made just before serving.

braised lamb shanks with sun-dried tomatoes

PREPARATION TIME 15 MINUTES • COOKING TIME 2 HOURS 30 MINUTES

3kg large lamb shanks
plain flour
2 tablespoons olive oil
12 baby onions (300g)
¹/₂ cup (55g) drained
   sun-dried tomatoes
¹/₂ cup (125ml) port
1¹/₂ cups (375ml) dry red wine
¹/₂ cup (125ml) chicken stock
2 tablespoons finely chopped
   fresh parsley

1 Toss lamb in flour; shake away excess flour. Heat oil in large baking dish; cook lamb, in batches, until browned all over. Drain on absorbent paper.

2 Return lamb to dish; add onions, tomatoes, port, wine and stock. Cover; cook in moderate oven about 2 hours or until lamb is tender.

3 Remove lamb from dish; keep warm. Simmer pan juices over heat until thickened slightly.

4 Serve lamb with pan juices; sprinkle with parsley.

SERVES 8

per serving 25g fat; 1832kJ
store Recipe can be made a day ahead and refrigerated, covered. Recipe suitable to freeze.

irish stew

PREPARATION TIME 15 MINUTES • COOKING TIME 1 HOUR 20 MINUTES

1/4 cup (60ml) vegetable oil
2kg lamb neck chops
1 medium leek (350g),
  chopped finely
3 large potatoes (900g),
  chopped coarsely
2 medium carrots (240g),
  chopped coarsely
1 tablespoon finely chopped
  fresh thyme
1 litre (4 cups) lamb or
  chicken stock

1 Heat half of the oil in large saucepan; cook chops, in batches, until browned lightly all over. Remove from pan.

2 Heat remaining oil in pan; cook leek, stirring, until just tender.

3 Add potato, carrot and thyme, then return chops to pan with stock; simmer, covered, about 1 hour or until chops are tender.

SERVES 8

per serving 22.1g fat; 1929kJ
store Recipe can be made a day ahead and refrigerated, covered. Recipe suitable to freeze.

lamb pot roast

PREPARATION TIME 20 MINUTES (plus marinating time) • COOKING TIME 2 HOURS

2 x 1kg boned rolled lamb shoulders
2 cloves garlic, crushed
2 fresh rosemary sprigs
1 teaspoon coarsely chopped fresh thyme
1 teaspoon grated orange rind
1 cup (250ml) dry red wine
1 teaspoon olive oil
4 bacon rashers (285g), chopped coarsely
370g spring onions, trimmed
1 tablespoon chicken stock powder
12 baby new potatoes (480g)
2 medium carrots (240g), halved
2 teaspoons cornflour
1 tablespoon water

1 Combine lamb, garlic, herbs, rind and wine in large bowl; cover, refrigerate several hours or overnight.

2 Remove lamb from marinade; reserve marinade. Pat lamb dry with absorbent paper; brush with oil.

3 Heat 3 litre (12-cup) deep, flameproof casserole dish; cook lamb until browned all over. Remove from dish. Add bacon and onion to dish; cook, stirring, until onion is browned lightly.

4 Return lamb to dish. Add reserved marinade and stock powder; cook, covered in moderate oven 45 minutes.

5 Add potatoes and carrot; cook, covered, about 1 hour or until lamb and vegetables are tender. Remove lamb and vegetables from dish.

6 Discard all but 2 cups (500ml) of the cooking liquid. Add blended cornflour and water to dish. Stir in cooking liquid; stir over heat until mixture boils and thickens slightly.

7 Serve sliced lamb and vegetables with sauce.

SERVES 8

per serving 16.7g fat; 1858kJ
store Recipe can be made a day ahead and refrigerated, covered.
Recipe suitable to freeze; thicken with cornflour just before serving.

minted lamb racks

PREPARATION TIME 20 MINUTES (plus marinating time) • COOKING TIME 1 HOUR 30 MINUTES

4 racks of lamb (3 cutlets each)
1¹/2 tablespoons vegetable oil
1 medium red onion (170g),
  chopped finely
2 trimmed sticks celery (150g),
  chopped finely
1 medium apple (150g),
  chopped finely
³/4 cup (180ml) beef stock
1 tablespoon finely chopped
  fresh mint
2 teaspoons finely chopped
  fresh sage

MARINADE
¹/2 cup (125ml) fruit chutney
¹/2 cup (125ml) dry white wine
2 cloves garlic, crushed
¹/2 teaspoon ground cumin
¹/2 teaspoon ground coriander

1 Combine lamb and marinade in large bowl; mix well. Cover; refrigerate several hours or overnight.

2 Drain lamb; reserve marinade. Heat half of the oil in 1.5 litre (6-cup) flameproof casserole dish; cook onion, celery and apple, stirring, until onion is soft. Remove from dish.

3 Heat remaining oil in dish; cook lamb until browned all over.

4 Return onion mixture to dish. Add stock, reserved marinade and herbs; bring to a boil. Cook, covered, in moderate oven about 1 hour or until lamb is tender. Cut lamb into cutlets before serving.

marinade Combine ingredients in medium bowl; mix well.

SERVES 4

per serving 16.3g fat; 1500kJ
store Recipe best marinated a day ahead and refrigerated, covered. Recipe suitable to freeze.

lamb and artichoke stew

PREPARATION TIME 30 MINUTES • COOKING TIME 1 HOUR 35 MINUTES

3 medium globe artichokes (800g)
1/4 cup (60ml) lemon juice
1/4 cup (60ml) olive oil
1 large brown onion (200g),
  sliced thinly
1.5kg diced lamb
plain flour
2 1/2 cups (625ml) chicken stock
1 teaspoon grated lemon rind
2 medium carrots (240g),
  sliced thickly
1 cup (150g) frozen broad beans,
  thawed, peeled
1 tablespoon tomato paste
1 tablespoon coarsely chopped
  fresh dill
3/4 cup (125g) seeded black olives

1 Remove tough outer leaves from artichokes; trim tips of remaining leaves with scissors. Cut artichokes in half; place artichokes and juice in large saucepan of boiling water. Simmer, uncovered, about 25 minutes or until tender; drain.

2 Meanwhile, heat 1 tablespoon of the oil in small saucepan; cook onion, stirring, until soft. Remove from pan.

3 Toss lamb in flour; shake away excess flour. Heat remaining oil in pan; cook lamb, in batches, until browned.

4 Return onion to pan with stock and rind; simmer, uncovered, 45 minutes, stirring occasionally.

5 Add carrots; simmer, uncovered, 10 minutes. Add beans and artichokes; simmer, uncovered, 15 minutes or until lamb and vegetables are tender.

6 Stir in paste, dill and olives.

SERVES 6

per serving 19.2g fat; 1986kJ
store Recipe can be made a day ahead and refrigerated, covered. Recipe suitable to freeze.

spiced apricot and lamb tagine

PREPARATION TIME 20 MINUTES • COOKING TIME 2 HOURS

1/4 cup (60ml) olive oil
1kg diced lamb
2 cloves garlic, crushed
1 large brown onion (200g), chopped finely
1/4 teaspoon ground cinnamon
1/2 teaspoon ground cumin
1/2 teaspoon ground ginger
1/2 teaspoon ground turmeric
3 cups (750ml) water
1 cinnamon stick
2 strips lemon rind
11/2 tablespoons honey
1 cup (150g) dried apricots
1/2 cup (80g) blanched almonds, toasted
2 tablespoons coarsely chopped fresh coriander
1 tablespoon sesame seeds, toasted

1 Heat oil in large saucepan; cook lamb, in batches, stirring, until browned. Remove from pan.

2 Add garlic, onion and ground spices to pan; cook, stirring, until onion is soft. Stir in the water, cinnamon stick and rind.

3 Return lamb to pan; simmer, covered, about 11/2 hours or until lamb is tender.

4 Add honey, apricots and nuts to lamb mixture; simmer, uncovered, 10 minutes or until apricots are tender. Discard cinnamon stick and rind; stir in coriander.

5 Serve sprinkled with sesame seeds.

SERVES 4

per serving 35.8g fat; 2815kJ
store Recipe can be made a day ahead and refrigerated, covered. Recipe suitable to freeze.

lamb with mushrooms and potatoes

PREPARATION TIME 25 MINUTES • COOKING TIME 1 HOUR

8 lamb chump chops (1kg)
plain flour
2 tablespoons vegetable oil
4 bacon rashers (285g),
    chopped coarsely
150g flat mushrooms, quartered
150g button mushrooms
1 clove garlic, crushed
1 cup (250ml) beef stock
1 tablespoon red wine vinegar
12 baby new potatoes (480g)
2 tablespoons coarsely chopped
    fresh parsley

1 Trim fat from chops. Toss chops in flour; shake away excess flour. Heat half of the oil in 3 litre (12-cup) flameproof casserole dish; cook chops, in batches, until browned. Remove from dish.

2 Heat remaining oil in dish; cook bacon, mushrooms and garlic, stirring, 5 minutes.

3 Return chops to dish. Add stock, vinegar and potatoes; bring to a boil. Cook, covered, in moderate oven about 45 minutes or until chops are tender.

4 Serve sprinkled with parsley.

SERVES 4

per serving 34.3g fat; 2599kJ
store Recipe can be made a day ahead and refrigerated, covered. Recipe suitable to freeze.

spicy coconut lamb

PREPARATION TIME 15 MINUTES • COOKING TIME 1 HOUR 45 MINUTES

40g butter
4 dried curry leaves
**2 medium brown onions (300g),
  sliced thickly**
1/2 teaspoon chilli powder
1 teaspoon ground turmeric
1 teaspoon ground cumin
2 teaspoons ground coriander
5 cloves garlic, crushed
3 teaspoons grated fresh ginger
1kg diced lamb
2 tablespoons brown vinegar
425g can tomatoes
2 1/2 cups (625ml) water
4 cardamom pods, bruised
1 cinnamon stick
2 strips lemon rind
**4 small potatoes (480g),
  chopped coarsely**
**4 finger eggplants (240g),
  chopped coarsely**
**1/4 cup (30g) packaged
  ground almonds**
3/4 cup (180ml) coconut milk

1 Heat butter in large saucepan; cook curry leaves onion, chilli powder, ground spices, garlic and ginger, stirring until fragrant.

2 Add lamb; stir until browned lightly. Add vinegar, undrained crushed tomatoes, water, cardamom, cinnamon and rind; simmer, covered, 30 minutes.

3 Add potatoes; simmer, covered, about 30 minutes or until lamb is tender.

4 Add eggplant to lamb mixture; simmer, uncovered, 30 minutes. Discard leaves, whole spices and rind; stir in nuts and coconut milk.

SERVES 6

per serving 21.2g fat; 1795kJ
store Recipe can be made a day ahead and refrigerated, covered.
Recipe suitable to freeze; stir in nuts and coconut milk after reheating.

lamb with madeira and olive sauce

PREPARATION TIME 15 MINUTES • COOKING TIME 1 HOUR 45 MINUTES

1 teaspoon vegetable oil
8 lamb drumsticks
4 medium brown onions (600g), chopped finely
8 cloves garlic, peeled
1/4 cup (30g) seeded black olives, quartered
2 tablespoons tomato paste
6 medium egg tomatoes (450g), halved
1 cup (250ml) beef stock
1/2 cup (125ml) madeira
2 teaspoons dried rosemary leaves

1 Heat oil in 3 litre (12-cup) flameproof casserole dish. Cook lamb, in batches, until browned all over; remove from dish. Add onion and garlic, to dish; cook, stirring, until onion is soft.

2 Return lamb to dish. Add olive, paste, tomato, stock, madeira and rosemary; cook, uncovered, in moderate oven 1 1/2 hours or until lamb is tender.

SERVES 8

per serving 25g fat; 1832kJ
store Recipe can be made a day ahead and refrigerated, covered. Recipe suitable to freeze.

lamb with redcurrant and red wine sauce

PREPARATION TIME 15 MINUTES • COOKING TIME 1 HOUR 45 MINUTES

2 tablespoons vegetable oil
1.5kg leg of lamb
4 medium carrots (480g),
  chopped coarsely
4 medium parsnips (500g),
  chopped coarsely
6 small brown onions
(480g), quartered
4 cloves garlic, crushed
3 bacon rashers (215g),
  chopped coarsely
2 tablespoons redcurrant jelly
2 tablespoons tomato paste
1 cup (250ml) dry red wine
1 beef stock cube, crumbled
1 tablespoon finely chopped
  fresh thyme

1 Heat oil in large saucepan; cook lamb until browned all over. Remove from pan.

2 Add carrot, parsnip, onion, garlic and bacon to pan; cook, stirring, until browned lightly.

3 Add remaining ingredients. Bring to a boil; return lamb to pan. Reduce heat; simmer, covered, about 1¼ hours or until tender.

4 Serve lamb sliced with sauce and vegetables.

SERVES 4

per serving 29g fat; 3025kJ

store Recipe can be made a day ahead and refrigerated, covered. Recipe suitable to freeze.

lancashire hot pot

PREPARATION TIME 15 MINUTES • COOKING TIME 3 HOURS

8 lamb neck chops (1kg)
3 medium brown onions
 (450g), sliced thinly
3 large potatoes (900g),
 sliced thinly
4 bacon rashers (285g),
 chopped finely
1³/4 cups (430ml) beef stock
30g butter, chopped coarsely

1 Trim fat from chops; place chops
 in 3 litre (12-cup) ovenproof
 casserole dish. Top with a layer
 of onion, potato and bacon.
 Repeat layering, ending with
 potatoes. Pour over stock; top
 with butter.

2 Cook, covered, in moderately
 slow oven 2 hours. Remove
 cover; cook about 1 hour or until
 chops are tender.

3 Serve with baby carrots,
 if desired.

SERVES 4

per serving 24.4g fat; 2537kJ
store Recipe best made just
before serving.

pork & veal

The many cuts of pork are transformed into sensational meals with these recipes including classics such as apple pork and prunes, as well as more contemporary offerings such as veal and prosciutto roll with caramelised onions.

veal cutlets with thyme and vegetables

PREPARATION TIME 30 MINUTES • COOKING TIME 1 HOUR 15 MINUTES

12 small veal cutlets (1.4kg)
1/4 cup (35g) plain flour
1 tablespoon cajun seasoning
2 tablespoons vegetable oil
2 cups (500ml) chicken stock
1/2 cup (125ml) dry white wine
10 spring onions, trimmed
2 teaspoons finely chopped fresh thyme
2 bay leaves
10 baby carrots
150g baby green beans, halved
100g fresh baby corn
1 tablespoon finely chopped fresh parsley

1 Toss cutlets in combined flour and cajun seasoning; shake away excess flour mixture. Reserve excess flour mixture.

2 Heat oil in large saucepan. Cook cutlets, in batches, until browned on both sides; remove from pan.

3 Stir reserved flour mixture into pan; stir over heat until bubbling. Remove from heat; gradually stir in stock and wine. Stir over heat until sauce boils and thickens.

4 Return cutlets to pan. Stir in onion, thyme and bay leaves; simmer, covered 20 minutes, stirring occasionally.

5 Stir in carrots, beans and corn; simmer, covered, about 15 minutes or until cutlets and vegetables are tender. Discard bay leaves; stir in parsley.

SERVES 6

per serving 12.8g fat; 1623kJ
store Recipe can be made a day ahead and refrigerated, covered. Recipe suitable to freeze.

veal with spinach and mushrooms

PREPARATION TIME 20 MINUTES • COOKING TIME 2 HOURS

1 tablespoon olive oil
1.5kg diced veal
2 medium leeks (700g),
   sliced thinly
2 teaspoons finely chopped
   fresh thyme
1/2 cup (125ml) dry white wine
2 small chicken stock cubes
425g can tomatoes
500g button mushrooms
1 medium red capsicum (200g),
   chopped finely
500g english spinach,
   chopped coarsely
1/4 cup finely shredded fresh basil

1 Heat oil in large saucepan; cook veal, in batches, stirring, until browned. Add leek and thyme; cook, stirring, until leek is soft.

2 Stir in wine, crumbled stock cubes, undrained crushed tomatoes, mushrooms and capsicum; simmer, covered, about 1 1/2 hours or until veal is very tender. Stir in spinach and basil just before serving.

3 Serve with rice, if desired.

SERVES 6

per serving 11.5g fat; 1685kJ
store Recipe can be made a day ahead and refrigerated, covered. Recipe suitable to freeze.

veal with eggplant, olives and capers

PREPARATION TIME 20 MINUTES • COOKING TIME 2 HOURS 30 MINUTES

1.5kg diced veal
plain flour
2 tablespoons olive oil
10 spring onions,
   trimmed, halved
4 cloves garlic, crushed
1 tablespoon drained capers,
   chopped finely
1 large eggplant (500g),
   chopped coarsely
10 medium tomatoes (1.3kg),
   chopped coarsely
1/4 cup (60ml) tomato paste
1 cup (250ml) dry white wine
2 teaspoons finely chopped
   fresh thyme
2 bay leaves
1/4 cup (40g) seeded
   black olives
2 tablespoons pine nuts, toasted
2 tablespoons finely chopped
   fresh mint leaves

1 Toss veal in flour; shake away excess flour. Heat oil in 3 litre (12-cup) flameproof casserole dish; cook veal, in batches, until browned. Remove from dish.

2 Cook onion, garlic, capers and eggplant in dish, stirring, 5 minutes.

3 Add veal, then stir in tomato, paste, wine, thyme and bay leaves.

4 Cook, covered, in moderate oven about 2 hours or until veal is tender. Discard bay leaves.

5 Serve topped with olives, nuts and mint.

SERVES 6

per serving 17.6g fat; 2068kJ
store Recipe can be made a day ahead and refrigerated, covered. Recipe suitable to freeze.

pork with beans and beer

PREPARATION TIME 20 MINUTES • COOKING TIME 2 HOURS 20 MINUTES

We used a dish with a base measuring 23cm, so the pork was covered with liquid during cooking. Any small white dried bean can be used.

3 cloves garlic, crushed
1/2 teaspoon freshly ground black pepper
1.8kg pork neck
1 tablespoon olive oil
3 bacon rashers (215g), chopped finely
2 medium brown onions (300g), sliced thinly
2 teaspoons caraway seeds
375ml can beer
1 cup (200g) dried haricot beans
11/2 cups (375ml) chicken stock
1/4 small (300g) white cabbage, shredded finely

1 Rub combined garlic and pepper all over pork. Secure pork with string at 2cm intervals to make an even shape.

2 Heat oil in 5 litre (20-cup) large flameproof casserole dish. Cook pork, turning, until browned all over. Remove from dish.

3 Cook bacon, onion and seeds in dish, stirring, until onion is soft and bacon browned lightly.

4 Return pork to dish. Add beer, beans and stock; simmer, covered, about 2 hours or until beans and pork are tender.

5 Remove pork from dish. Add cabbage; cook, stirring, until just wilted.

SERVES 8

per serving 13g fat; 1754kJ
store Recipe can be made a day ahead and refrigerated, covered.
Recipe suitable to freeze.

veal fricassee

PREPARATION TIME 10 MINUTES • COOKING TIME 1 HOUR

80g butter
1.5kg diced veal
2 large brown onions (400g),
    sliced thickly
1/2 cup (75g) plain flour
1/4 cup (60ml) dry white wine
3 cups (750ml) chicken stock
1 teaspoon cracked black pepper
1 tablespoon coarsely chopped
    fresh parsley
2 teaspoons coarsely chopped
    fresh thyme
3 egg yolks
1/2 cup (125ml) cream
1/4 teaspoon ground nutmeg
2 teaspoons lemon juice

1 Heat butter in large saucepan; cook veal and onion, covered, until onion is soft. Stir in flour; cook, stirring, 3 minutes.

2 Stir in wine, stock, pepper and herbs; simmer, covered, about 45 minutes or until veal is tender. Just before serving, stir in combined egg yolks, cream, nutmeg and juice; stir until hot.

SERVES 6

per serving 31.1g fat; 2480kJ

store Recipe can be prepared a day ahead and refrigerated, covered. Recipe suitable to freeze.

ragout of veal and mushrooms

PREPARATION TIME 15 MINUTES • COOKING TIME 1 HOUR 15 MINUTES

1.5kg diced veal
plain flour
20g butter
1¹/₂ tablespoons olive oil
1 medium leek (350g),
  chopped finely
2 cloves garlic, crushed
1 cup (250ml) dry white wine
1 litre (4 cups) water
2 tablespoons tomato paste
1 teaspoon ground black pepper
300g button mushrooms,
  sliced thinly
¹/₃ cup (80ml) cream

1 Toss veal in flour; shake away excess flour. Heat butter and oil in large saucepan; cook veal, in batches, until browned lightly. Drain on absorbent paper.

2 Add leek and garlic to pan; cook, covered, until leek is soft. Add wine; cook, stirring, until liquid reduce by a half.

3 Return veal to pan. Add the water, paste and pepper; simmer, covered, 30 minutes.

4 Add mushrooms; simmer, uncovered, about 20 minutes or until liquid has thickened slightly. Stir in cream just before serving.

SERVES 6

per serving 19.5g fat; 1946kJ
store Recipe can be made a day ahead and refrigerated, covered. Recipe suitable to freeze.

apples, pork and prunes

PREPARATION TIME 25 MINUTES • COOKING TIME 1 HOUR 30 MINUTES

2 tablespoons vegetable oil
2 small leeks (400g), sliced thinly
4 forequarter pork chops (1.75kg)
plain flour
1 litre (4 cups) chicken stock
1/2 cup (100g) long-grain rice
4 medium apples (600g), sliced thickly
1 cup (170g) seeded prunes
2 tablespoons coarsely chopped fresh sage

1 Heat one-third of the oil in 2.5 litre (10-cup) flameproof casserole dish; cook leek, stirring, until soft. Remove from dish.

2 Trim fat and bone from chops; cut pork into 5cm pieces. Toss pork in flour; shake away excess flour.

3 Heat remaining oil in dish; cook pork, stirring, until browned. Add leek and stock to dish; cook, covered, in moderate oven 45 minutes.

4 Remove dish from oven; skim off any fat. Stir in rice, apple, prunes and half of the sage; cook, covered, about 20 minutes or until pork is tender.

5 Serve sprinkled with remaining sage.

SERVES 4

per serving 22.7g fat; 2978kJ
store Recipe can be made a day ahead and refrigerated, covered. Recipe suitable to freeze.

veal and prosciutto roll with caramelised onions

PREPARATION TIME 25 MINUTES • COOKING TIME 1 HOUR 30 MINUTES

2 cloves garlic, crushed
2 teaspoons finely chopped fresh sage
2 teaspoons finely chopped fresh thyme
1 teaspoon ground black pepper
1.5kg shoulder of veal, boned
3 slices (45g) prosciutto
2 tablespoons olive oil
1/2 cup (125ml) dry red wine
11/2 cups (375ml) beef stock

CARAMELISED ONIONS
1 tablespoon olive oil
30g butter
4 large brown onions (800g), sliced thinly
1 teaspoon finely chopped fresh sage
1 cup (160g) seeded black olives

1 Combine garlic, herbs and pepper in small bowl; mix well. Rub garlic mixture all over cut side of veal; top with prosciutto. Roll up firmly; secure with string at 2cm intervals.

2 Heat oil in large baking dish; cook veal in dish until browned all over. Pour over wine and stock; cook, covered, in moderately hot oven about 11/4 hours or until veal is tender.

3 Remove veal from dish; cover, keep warm. Simmer pan juices over heat until reduced by a half.

4 Serve veal with pan juices and caramelised onions.

caramelised onions Heat oil and butter in medium saucepan; cook onion and sage, stirring, over low heat about 20 minutes or until browned and caramelised. Add olives; stir until hot.

SERVES 6

per serving 20.2g fat; 2044kJ

store Veal can be prepared a day ahead and refrigerated, covered; caramelised onions best cooked just before serving.

hungarian-style goulash

PREPARATION TIME 25 MINUTES • COOKING TIME 1 HOUR 30 MINUTES

1kg forequarter veal,
   chopped coarsely
1 tablespoon paprika
2 tablespoons plain flour
2 teaspoons caraway seeds
1 tablespoon vegetable oil
20g butter
1 medium brown onion (150g),
   chopped finely
1 cup (250ml) beef stock
2 x 425g cans tomatoes
1 tablespoon tomato paste
3 medium potatoes (600g),
   chopped coarsely
2 teaspoons coarsely chopped
   fresh oregano

1 Toss veal in combined paprika,
   flour and seeds; shake away
   excess flour mixture.

2 Heat oil and butter in large
   saucepan; cook veal, in batches,
   stirring, until browned. Remove
   from pan. Add onion to pan;
   cook, stirring until soft.

3 Return veal to pan with stock,
   undrained crushed tomatoes
   and paste; simmer, covered,
   30 minutes. Add potato; simmer,
   covered, about 30 minutes or
   until veal and potato are tender.

4 Remove cover; simmer about
   5 minutes or until thickened
   slightly. Stir in oregano.

SERVES 6

per serving 10.7g fat; 1504kJ

store Recipe can be made a day
ahead and refrigerated, covered.
Recipe suitable to freeze.

ham and vegetables

PREPARATION TIME 25 MINUTES • COOKING TIME 45 MINUTES

40g butter
2 ham hocks (1.5kg)
$1/3$ cup (80ml) dry red wine
2 cups (500ml) chicken stock
2 medium potatoes (400g), chopped coarsely
1 medium brown onion (150g), chopped coarsely
3 finger eggplants (180g), chopped coarsely
1 small swede (150g), chopped coarsely
300g pumpkin, chopped coarsely
1 medium carrot (120g), chopped coarsely
$1/2$ cup (125ml) tomato puree
1 large zucchini (150g), chopped coarsely
150g button mushrooms, halved
1 tablespoon coarsely chopped fresh basil

1 Heat butter in large saucepan; cook ham hocks until browned lightly.

2 Add wine and stock. Cover; simmer about 1 hour until ham is tender.

3 Add potato, onion, eggplant, swede, pumpkin, carrot and tomato
   puree; simmer, uncovered 10 minutes. Add zucchini, mushrooms and basil;
   simmer, covered, about 15 minutes or until vegetables are tender.

4 Remove ham from bones and serve with vegetables and sauce.

SERVES 6

per serving 13.5g fat; 1355kJ
store Recipe best made just before serving.

88

braised veal rolls with pasta and olives

PREPARATION TIME 35 MINUTES • COOKING TIME 1 HOUR

Any small soup pasta can be used.

4 large red capsicums (1.4kg)
250g english spinach
8 veal steaks (900g)
1/4 cup (60ml) olive oil
2 medium brown onions (300g),
   chopped finely
2 cloves garlic, crushed

425g can tomato puree
1/3 cup (80ml) dry red wine
2 teaspoons brown sugar
1/2 cup (100g) stellettine pasta
3/4 cup (120g) seeded black olives
2 tablespoons shredded fresh basil

1 Quarter capsicums; remove seeds and membranes. Grill capsicum, skin side up, until skin blisters and blackens; peel away skin.

2 Place spinach leaves over each veal steak; top with capsicum. Roll veal tightly; secure with toothpicks.

3 Heat 2 tablespoons of the oil in large saucepan. Cook veal, in batches, until browned all over; drain on absorbent paper. Heat remaining oil in pan; cook onion and garlic, stirring, until onion is soft.

4 Add puree, wine, sugar and veal; simmer, covered, 15 minutes. Add pasta and olives; simmer, covered, about 7 minutes or until pasta is tender.

5 Serve veal sliced with sauce, sprinkled with basil.

SERVES 8

per serving 10.3g fat; 1324kJ
store Recipe best made just before serving.

osso bucco

PREPARATION TIME 20 MINUTES • COOKING TIME 3 HOURS

12 osso bucco (1.5kg)
plain flour
2 tablespoons olive oil
2 medium brown onions
   (300g), sliced thinly
4 cloves garlic, crushed
2 x 425g cans tomatoes
1/2 cup (125ml) dry white wine
1 cup (250ml) beef stock
1 bay leaf
1 tablespoon coarsely chopped
   fresh thyme
1 tablespoon coarsely chopped
   fresh oregano
2 tablespoons coarsely chopped
   fresh parsley

1 Toss veal in flour; shake away excess flour. Heat oil in large saucepan; cook veal, in batches, until browned all over. Drain on absorbent paper.

2 Add onion and garlic to pan; cook, stirring, until onion is soft.

3 Return veal to pan. Add undrained crushed tomatoes, wine, stock, bay leaf, thyme and oregano; simmer, covered 1 1/2 hours, stirring occasionally.

4 Remove cover; simmer about 1 hour or until veal is very tender. Discard bay leaf; serve osso bucco sprinkled with parsley.

SERVES 6

per serving 9.6g fat; 1136kJ
store Recipe can be made a day ahead and refrigerated, covered. Recipe suitable to freeze.

seafood

Universally popular, seafood has the built-in advantage of a brief cooking time, making it a great ally of the busy cook. Start with the catch of the day and make the most of it with these recipes which utilise fish, prawns, mussels, octopus and squid.

quick and easy prawn curry

PREPARATION TIME 20 MINUTES • COOKING TIME 30 MINUTES

2kg uncooked large prawns
1 tablespoon peanut oil
10 green onions, chopped finely
1 clove garlic, crushed
3 trimmed sticks celery (225g), sliced thinly
1$^1/_2$ tablespoons green curry paste
$^1/_2$ cup (125ml) fish stock
$^1/_2$ cup (125ml) water
400ml can coconut milk
2 tablespoons fresh coriander leaves

1 Shell and devein prawns, leaving tails intact.

2 Heat oil in large saucepan; cook onion and garlic, stirring, until onion is soft. Add celery and paste; cook, stirring, 2 minutes.

3 Stir in combined stock, water and half of the coconut milk; simmer, uncovered, 15 minutes. Add prawns to pan; simmer, stirring, about 5 minutes or until prawns are tender.

4 Add remaining coconut milk. Stir until heated through; do not boil. Sprinkle with coriander just before serving.

SERVES 4

per serving 29.6g fat; 2145kJ
store Recipe best made just before serving.

mixed seafood coconut curry

PREPARATION TIME 30 MINUTES • COOKING TIME 20 MINUTES

200g small mussels
300g uncooked medium prawns
150g squid hood
2 teaspoons vegetable oil
1 medium brown onion (150g),
    sliced thinly
2 cloves garlic, crushed
1 teaspoon grated fresh ginger
1 teaspoon sambal oelek
1/4 teaspoon belacan
1 tablespoon mild curry powder
1/2 teaspoon ground turmeric
2³/4 cups (680ml) coconut milk
1/4 cup (60ml) water
1 tablespoon tamarind sauce
150g green beans, halved
1kg boneless white fish fillets,
    chopped coarsely
2 medium tomatoes (260g),
    chopped coarsely
2 teaspoons coarsely chopped
    fresh coriander

1 Scrub mussels; remove beards.
  Shell and devein prawns, leaving
  tails intact.

2 Score inside surface of squid; cut
  into 3cm pieces.

3 Heat oil in large saucepan; cook
  onion, garlic, ginger, sambal
  oelek, belacan, curry powder and
  turmeric, stirring, until fragrant.

4 Stir in coconut milk, the water,
  tamarind and beans; bring to
  a boil.

5 Add all seafood; reduce heat.
  Simmer, uncovered, about
  5 minutes or until seafood
  is tender; stir in tomato and
  coriander. Stir until
  heated through.

SERVES 4

per serving 44.6g fat; 3126kJ
store Recipe best made just
before serving.

fish korma curry

PREPARATION TIME 15 MINUTES • COOKING TIME 50 MINUTES

30g ghee
2 medium brown onions (300g),
   chopped finely
500g white sweet potato,
   chopped coarsely
1/3 cup (80ml) korma curry paste
1 cup (250ml) cream
1 cup (250ml) water
1.2kg firm white fish fillets,
   chopped coarsely
1 tablespoon finely chopped
   fresh coriander
250g green beans, halved
250g cherry tomatoes

1 Heat ghee in large saucepan; cook onion, stirring, until just tender. Add sweet potato and paste; cook, stirring, 3 minutes.

2 Add cream and the water; simmer, covered, 30 minutes.

3 Add fish, coriander, beans and tomatoes. Stir gently; simmer, covered, about 10 minutes or until fish is tender.

SERVES 6

per serving 32.6g fat; 3249kJ
store Recipe best made just before serving.

quick lemon grass and coconut fish stew

PREPARATION TIME 20 MINUTES (plus standing time)
COOKING TIME 30 MINUTES

250g dried egg noodles
8 dried shiitake mushrooms
1 tablespoon vegetable oil
2 teaspoons grated fresh ginger
2 tablespoons finely chopped fresh lemon grass
1/2 teaspoon five spice powder
1 teaspoon ground turmeric
1 teaspoon sambal oelek
400ml can coconut cream
1/4 cup (60ml) chicken stock
1kg boneless white fish fillets, chopped coarsely
400g baby bok choy, quartered
4 green onions, chopped finely

1 Add noodles to large saucepan of boiling water. Boil, uncovered, until just tender; drain.

2 Place mushrooms in large heatproof bowl; cover with boiling water. Stand 20 minutes; drain mushrooms. Discard stems; slice caps.

3 Heat oil in large saucepan; cook ginger, lemon grass, spices, sambal oelek and mushrooms, stirring, until fragrant. Add coconut cream and stock; bring to a boil. Add fish; reduce heat. Cook covered, about 10 minutes or until fish is just tender.

4 Stir in bok choy, onion and noodles; reheat gently.

SERVES 6

per serving 23g fat; 2143kJ
store Recipe best made just before serving.

seafood casserole

PREPARATION TIME 30 MINUTES • COOKING TIME 45 MINUTES

1kg small mussels
1kg uncooked prawns
500g calamari hoods
500g uncooked lobster tail
1 tablespoon olive oil
1 medium leek (350g),
   sliced thinly
4 cloves garlic, crushed
425g can tomatoes
3/4 cup (180ml) dry white wine
1/4 cup (60ml) sweet sherry
2 cups (500ml) fish stock
pinch saffron threads
2 medium carrots (240g),
   chopped finely
1/3 cup finely chopped
   fresh parsley
1 tablespoon finely chopped
   fresh thyme
350g scallops

1 Scrub mussels; remove beards.
  Shell and devein prawns, leaving
  tails intact; cut calamari open.
  Score inside surface; cut into
  6cm pieces. Shell lobster tail;
  cut lobster meat into 5cm pieces.

2 Heat oil in large saucepan; cook
  leek and garlic, stirring, until
  leek is soft.

3 Add undrained crushed tomatoes,
  wine, sherry, stock, saffron,
  carrot and herbs; simmer,
  covered, 30 minutes.

4 Add mussels; simmer, covered,
  2 minutes. Add prawns, calamari
  and lobster pieces; simmer,
  covered, about 2 minutes. Add
  the scallops; simmer, uncovered,
  about 2 minutes or until seafood
  is just cooked. Discard any
  unopened mussels.

SERVES 6

per serving 6.7g fat; 1523kJ
store Recipe best made just
before serving.

octopus and squid casserole

PREPARATION TIME 20 MINUTES • COOKING TIME 1 HOUR 20 MINUTES

1kg baby octopus
500g squid hoods
1 tablespoon olive oil
2 cloves garlic, crushed
1/2 teaspoon sambal oelek
20 baby onions (500g)
1 teaspoon finely chopped
fresh thyme
1 teaspoon finely chopped
fresh oregano
2 teaspoons grated fresh ginger
1 teaspoon grated lime rind
2 x 425g cans tomatoes
1 teaspoon brown sugar
1/2 cup (80g) seeded black olives

1 Discard heads and beaks from octopus; cut octopus in half. Cut squid hoods into 2cm rings.

2 Heat oil in large saucepan; cook garlic, sambal oelek, onions, herbs, ginger and rind, stirring, 2 minutes. Add seafood, undrained crushed tomatoes and sugar; simmer, covered, 30 minutes.

3 Remove cover; simmer about 45 minutes or until seafood is tender and sauce thickened slightly. Stir in olives.

SERVES 6

per serving 5.1g fat; 829kJ
store Recipe can be made a day ahead and refrigerated, covered. Recipe suitable to freeze.

vegetarian

Turn versatile vegetables into substantial main meals with this selection including curries, casseroles and a gumbo. The addition of beans, lentils and chickpeas makes for some hearty offerings along with many other satisfying combinations.

red lentil and vegetable stew

PREPARATION TIME 25 MINUTES • COOKING TIME 45 MINUTES

4 medium zucchini (480g)
4 finger eggplants (240g)
1 medium red capsicum (200g)
2 tablespoons olive oil
2 cloves garlic, crushed
1 medium leek (350g), sliced thinly
1 teaspoon caraway seeds
1 teaspoon cumin seeds
2 x 425g cans tomatoes
1/3 cup (80ml) dry red wine
1 teaspoon brown sugar
1/4 cup (60ml) tomato paste
1 cup (200g) red lentils
2 cups (500ml) vegetable stock
1 tablespoon finely chopped fresh basil

1 Halve zucchini and eggplants lengthways. Quarter capsicum; remove seeds and membranes.

2 Heat 1 tablespoon of the oil heated grill plate (or grill or barbecue); cook vegetables, in batches, until browned on both sides. Remove from pan.

3 Heat remaining oil in large saucepan; cook garlic, leek and seeds, stirring, until leek is soft. Add undrained crushed tomatoes, wine, sugar, paste and lentils; simmer, uncovered, 5 minutes.

4 Stir in stock, basil and vegetables; simmer, uncovered, about 15 minutes or until vegetables are tender.

SERVES 4

per serving 13.6g fat; 1215kJ
store Recipe can be made a day ahead and refrigerated, covered.

spicy okra, corn and capsicum gumbo

PREPARATION TIME 30 MINUTES • COOKING TIME 1 HOUR

800g okra
1¹/₂ tablespoons olive oil
2 medium brown onions
   (300g), chopped coarsely
4 cloves garlic, crushed
1¹/₂ teaspoons cajun seasoning
1 teaspoon ground cumin
¹/₄ teaspoon cayenne pepper
3 trimmed sticks celery (225g),
chopped coarsely
2 large green capsicums (700g),
chopped coarsely
2 large red capsicums (700g),
   chopped coarsely
2 fresh trimmed corn cobs,
   (500g) chopped coarsely
10 baby carrots,
   chopped coarsely
2 cups (500ml) vegetable stock
2 x 425g cans tomatoes
2 tablespoons
   worcestershire sauce
¹/₂ cup (100g) basmati rice
¹/₄ cup finely chopped
   fresh parsley

1 Trim stems from okra;
   discard stems.

2 Heat oil in large heavy-based
   saucepan; cook onion, garlic
   and spices, stirring, until onion
   is soft. Add celery, capsicums,
   corn, carrot, stock, undrained
   crushed tomatoes and sauce;
   simmer, covered, 30 minutes.

3 Add rice and okra; simmer,
   covered, about 25 minutes or
   until rice is tender.

4 Serve sprinkled with parsley.

SERVES 6

per serving 7.1g fat; 1323kJ
store Recipe can be made a day
ahead and refrigerated, covered.
Recipe suitable to freeze.

capsicum casserole with zucchini and beans

PREPARATION TIME 35 MINUTES (plus standing time) • COOKING TIME 1 HOUR 45 MINUTES

1/2 cup (100g) dried borlotti beans
4 medium red capsicums (800g)
4 medium zucchini (480g),
  chopped finely
4 baby onions (100g), quartered
200g green beans, halved
310g can chickpeas, rinsed, drained
2 tablespoons olive oil
1/4 cup (20g) parmesan
  cheese flakes

TOMATO SAUCE
2 x 425g cans tomatoes
1 tablespoon balsamic vinegar
1/2 teaspoon brown sugar
1/4 cup finely shredded fresh basil

1 Place borlotti beans in large bowl; cover with water. Cover; stand overnight. Drain borlotti beans. Add to large saucepan of boiling water; reduce heat. Simmer, uncovered, about 20 minutes or until tender; drain.

2 Halve capsicums lengthways; remove seeds and membranes. Place capsicum, cut side up, in 3 litre (12-cup) shallow ovenproof dish.

3 Combine borlotti beans, zucchini, onion, green beans, chickpeas and oil in large bowl. Mix well; spoon into capsicum. Pour over tomato sauce; cook, covered, in moderate oven 1 hour. Remove cover; cook about 15 minutes or until capsicum is tender. Serve topped with cheese flakes.

tomato sauce Combine undrained crushed tomatoes, vinegar and sugar in large saucepan; simmer, uncovered, about 5 minutes or until sauce is thickened slightly. Stir in basil.

SERVES 4

per serving 13.2g fat; 1274kJ

store Capsicum and sauce can be prepared a day ahead and refrigerated, covered separately.

grilled eggplants, tomato and chickpeas

PREPARATION TIME 20 MINUTES • COOKING TIME 1 HOUR

2 medium eggplants (600g), sliced thickly
2 tablespoons olive oil
10 spring onions (250g), trimmed
2 cloves garlic, crushed
3 trimmed sticks celery (225g), sliced thinly
2 x 310g cans chickpeas, rinsed, drained
4 large tomatoes (1kg), peeled, chopped fienly
1/4 cup finely chopped fresh parsley
1/4 cup finely chopped fresh oregano
1 tablespoon tomato paste
150g italian beans, trimmed, halved

1 Place eggplant slices on greased oven tray; brush lightly with about half of the oil. Grill until browned on both sides.

2 Heat remaining oil in 3 litre (12-cup) flameproof casserole dish; cook onion, stirring, until onion is browned lightly.

3 Stir in eggplant, garlic, celery, chickpeas, tomato and herbs. Cook, covered, in moderate oven about 45 minutes or until vegetables are tender.

4 Remove from oven; stir in paste and beans.

SERVES 4

per serving 12.4g fat; 1128kJ
store Recipe can be made a day ahead and refrigerated, covered.
Recipe suitable to freeze.

vindaloo vegetables

PREPARATION TIME 25 MINUTES • COOKING TIME 50 MINUTES

1 tablespoon vegetable oil
2 medium brown onions (300g),
   chopped coarsely
2 cloves garlic, crushed
1/4 cup (60ml) vindaloo
   curry paste
12 baby new potatoes (480g)
800g pumpkin, chopped coarsely
1 large red capsicum (350g),
   chopped coarsely
3 medium carrots (360g),
   chopped coarsely
1/4 medium cauliflower
   (400g), chopped coarsely
11/2 cups (375ml)
   vegetable stock
425ml can coconut milk
2 dried lime leaves
1/3 cup (50g) dried currants
3 fresh trimmed corn cobs
   (750g), chopped coarsely
3 medium zucchini (350g),
   chopped coarsely
400g broccoli, chopped coarsely
1/4 cup (35g) chopped roasted
   unsalted peanuts

1 Heat oil in large saucepan; cook
   onion and garlic, stirring, until
   onion is soft. Add curry paste;
   cook, stirring, until fragrant.

2 Add potatoes, pumpkin, capsicum,
   carrot, cauliflower, stock, coconut
   milk, lime leaves and currants;
   simmer, covered, 20 minutes.

3 Stir in corn, zucchini and
   broccoli; simmer, covered, about
   20 minutes or until vegetables
   are tender.

4 Serve sprinkled with peanuts.

SERVES 4

per serving 36.5xg fat; 3422kJ
store Recipe can be made a day
ahead and refrigerated, covered.
Recipe suitable to freeze.

kumara and potatoes in peanut coconut sauce

PREPARATION TIME 20 MINUTES • COOKING TIME 30 MINUTES

2 medium kumara (800g)
1 tablespoon peanut oil
2 medium brown onions (300g),
   sliced thinly
2 cloves garlic, crushed
1 teaspoon grated fresh ginger
1/2 teaspoon sambal oelek
1 tablespoon mild curry powder
1 teaspoon ground cumin
1 teaspoon ground coriander
1 tablespoon soy sauce
1/2 cup (130g) smooth
   peanut butter
21/2 cups (625ml) vegetable stock
1 cup (250ml) coconut milk
12 baby new potatoes
   (480g), halved
3/4 cup (150g) red lentils
1 tablespoon finely chopped
   fresh coriander

1 Cut kumara into 3cm pieces. Heat oil in large saucepan; cook onion, garlic, ginger, sambal oelek and spices, stirring, until fragrant.

2 Add sauce, peanut butter, stock, coconut milk and potato; simmer, covered, 5 minutes.

3 Add lentils and kumara; simmer, covered, stirring often, about 20 minutes or until vegetables are tender.

4 Serve sprinkled with fresh coriander.

SERVES 4

per serving 36.3g fat; 3026kJ
store Recipe can be made a day ahead and refrigerated, covered.

special occasions

Do-ahead dishes are a blessing for the busy host. This selection of special occasion fare uses imaginative combinations based on turkey, rabbit, duck and quail. Best of all, they can be made in advance and reheated just before serving, leaving the cook free to enjoy the guests' company.

anise and ginger braised duck

PREPARATION TIME 30 MINUTES (plus refrigerating time) • COOKING TIME 2 HOURS

1.7kg duck
1/4 cup (60ml) sweet sherry
1 cup (250ml) water
2 tablespoons soy sauce
4 cloves garlic, sliced thinly
3cm piece fresh ginger,
  sliced thinly
3 star anise
1 teaspoon sambal oelek
1 teaspoon cornflour
2 teaspoons water, extra

duck pieces cut for recipe

1 Using knife or poultry shears, cut down either side of duck backbone; discard. Cut duck in half through breastbone, then cut each half into two pieces. Trim excess fat from duck, leaving skin intact.

2 Place duck pieces in single layer, skin side down, in large saucepan; cook over low heat about 10 minutes or until skin is crisp. Drain on absorbent paper.

3 Place duck in clean saucepan. Add sherry, the water, sauce, garlic, ginger, star anise and sambal oelek; simmer, covered, about 1 1/2 hours or until duck is very tender. Turn duck halfway through cooking. Cover undrained duck mixture; refrigerate overnight.

4 Next day, discard fat layer from surface; place duck mixture in large saucepan. Cover; cook over low heat until duck is heated through. Remove duck from pan; keep warm.

5 Strain liquid into small saucepan; stir in blended cornflour and extra water. Stir over heat until mixture boils and thickens slightly.

6 Serve sauce over duck with steamed bok choy, if desired.

SERVES 4

per serving 39g fat; 2117kJ
store Recipe must be made a day ahead and refrigerated, covered. Recipe suitable to freeze.

braised turkey with mushrooms and apricots

PREPARATION TIME 30 MINUTES • COOKING TIME 1 HOUR

3kg turkey
plain flour
1/4 cup (60ml) olive oil
2 medium brown onions
   (300g), sliced thickly
1 clove garlic, crushed
250g button mushrooms
1 cup (150g) dried apricots

1 medium red capsicum
   (200g), sliced thickly
1/4 cup (60ml) dry white wine
2 cups (500ml) chicken stock
425ml can apricot nectar
1 tablespoon finely chopped
   fresh parsley

1 Using a knife or poultry shears, cut down either side of turkey backbone; discard backbone. Cut turkey in half through breastbone, then cut each half into even-sized pieces.

2 Toss turkey pieces in flour; shake away excess flour. Heat half of the oil in large saucepan; cook turkey, in batches, until browned all over. Drain on absorbent paper.

3 Heat remaining oil in pan; cook onion, garlic, mushrooms, apricots and capsicum, stirring, until onion is soft. Add wine; cook, stirring, until most of the liquid has evaporated.

4 Return turkey to pan; add stock and nectar. Stir until combined; simmer, covered, about 40 minutes or until turkey is tender.

5 Serve sprinkled with parsley.

SERVES 8

per serving 21g fat; 1953kJ
store Recipe can be made a day ahead and refrigerated, covered. Recipe suitable to freeze.

turkey pieces cut for recipe

creamy rabbit with fresh tarragon

PREPARATION TIME 20 MINUTES • COOKING TIME 2 HOURS 30 MINUTES

1.7kg rabbit cutlets
plain flour
2 tablespoons olive oil
5 cloves garlic, crushed
2 tablespoons brown sugar
10 spring onions (250g),
** trimmed, halved**
1 tablespoon white
** wine vinegar**
1 cup (250ml) dry white wine
1 cup (250ml) chicken stock
3 tablespoons finely chopped
** fresh tarragon**
¹/₂ cup (125ml) cream

1 Toss rabbit in flour; shake away excess flour. Heat oil in 3 litre (12-cup) flameproof casserole dish; cook rabbit, in batches, until browned on both sides. Drain on absorbent paper

2 Add garlic to dish; cook, stirring, until browned lightly. Add sugar, onion and vinegar; cook 5 minutes.

3 Stir in wine, stock and 2 tablespoons of the tarragon; bring to a boil. Add rabbit; cook, covered, in moderate oven about 2 hours or until rabbit is tender. Remove rabbit and onion from dish; keep warm.

4 Transfer cooking liquid to clean saucepan; bring to a boil. Reduce heat; simmer, uncovered, 5 minutes.

5 Stir in cream and remaining tarragon; stir until hot. Serve sauce over rabbit.

SERVES 6

per serving 21g fat; 1684kJ

store Recipe best made just before serving.

Recipe suitable to freeze; stir in cream and tarragon when reheating.

confit of duck with peach chutney

PREPARATION TIME 1 HOUR (plus refrigerating time) • COOKING TIME 2 HOURS 30 MINUTES (plus cooling time)

A confit is a method of preserving where goose, duck, turkey or pork is cooked slowly in its own fat. Here, we have supplemented duck fat with lard. Choose a large, shallow ovenproof dish so that duck pieces can be packed in a single layer and covered with the fat mixture at all stages. The fat mixture may be re-used for a similar recipe, if it is clarified before re-using.

2 x 1.7kg ducks
1 tablespoon sea salt
2 tablespoons finely chopped
   fresh thyme
4 cloves garlic, flattened
12 black peppercorns
500g lard, chopped coarsely

PEACH CHUTNEY

4 medium peaches (800g)
1 medium brown onion (150g),
   chopped finely
1 tablespoon finely chopped
   fresh thyme
1 cup (200g) firmly packed
   brown sugar
3/4 cup (180ml) white
   wine vinegar
1 large apple (150g),
   chopped coarsely
2 tablespoons chopped dried figs
1/4 teaspoon ground ginger

1 Place one duck on board, breast side up. Cut thigh and leg portions from duck. Cut along one side of breastbone, cutting down alongside the wish bone. Slide knife between breast and bone; remove breast (with skin) from bone. Repeat with other side. Repeat procedure with remaining duck; discard carcasses.

2 Remove skin and fat from legs. Discard skin; reserve fat. Place duck pieces in shallow ovenproof dish; sprinkle with salt, thyme, garlic and peppercorns. Cover; refrigerate 30 minutes.

3 Combine lard and reserved duck fat in large saucepan; heat until melted. Add duck pieces; bring to a boil. Remove from heat.

4 Return duck pieces to shallow ovenproof dish in a single layer; carefully pour over hot fat mixture, making sure duck pieces are completely covered. Cook, covered, in moderately slow oven about 2 hours or until duck is very tender; cool to room temperature. Discard garlic; refrigerate duck, covered, for at least 3 days before serving.

5 To serve, remove duck pieces as required; remove as much excess fat as possible. Place duck on oven tray; grill until heated through and skin is crisp.

6 Serve with peach chutney.

peach chutney Add peaches to large saucepan of boiling water. Boil, uncovered, 1 minute; drain. Rinse under cold water; drain. Peel away skins; halve peaches. Discard stones; chop peaches coarsely. Combine peaches with remaining ingredients in medium saucepan; stir over heat, without boiling, until sugar is dissolved. Bring to a boil; reduce heat. Simmer, uncovered, stirring occasionally, about 30 minutes or until mixture is thick. Pour mixture into 500ml (2-cup) hot sterilised jar; seal while hot.

SERVES 6

per serving 74.1g fat; 4210kJ
store Duck can be made one month ahead and refrigerated, covered; peach chutney can be made three months ahead and stored in a cool, dark place.

cutting leg portions from duck

removing duck breast from bone

rabbit with port, orange and sage

PREPARATION TIME 20 MINUTES • COOKING TIME 2 HOURS

1.5kg rabbit pieces
plain flour
2 tablespoons vegetable oil
2 large brown onions
   (400g), quartered
4 cloves garlic, crushed
1/2 cup (125ml) orange juice
1/2 cup (125ml) port
1 cup (250ml) dry red wine
2 tablespoons redcurrant jelly
1 medium orange (180g),
   sliced thinly
10 small fresh sage leaves
1 cup (250ml) chicken stock

1 Toss rabbit pieces in flour; shake away excess flour. Heat half of the oil in 1.75 litre (7-cup) flameproof casserole dish; cook rabbit, in batches, until browned on both sides. Remove from dish.

2 Heat remaining oil in dish; cook onion and garlic, stirring, until onion is soft.

3 Add rabbit and remaining ingredients; cook, covered, in moderately slow oven about 1 1/2 hours or until rabbit is tender.

SERVES 6

per serving 11.4g fat; 1549kJ
store Recipe can be made a day ahead and refrigerated, covered. Recipe suitable to freeze.

roast quail with sage and bacon

PREPARATION TIME 20 MINUTES • COOKING TIME 1 HOUR

12 quail
12 fresh sage leaves
12 bacon rashers (860g)
2 tablespoons olive oil
2 cloves garlic, crushed
1 small leek (200g),
  chopped finely
300g button mushrooms,
  sliced thinly
1 tablespoon plain flour
1/4 cup (60ml) dry white wine
3/4 cup (180ml)
  chicken stock
425g can tomato puree
1 teaspoon brown sugar
1 tablespoon finely chopped
  fresh parsley

1 Tuck wings under quail; bend legs back to insert into wings. Wrap each quail in sage and bacon; secure with toothpicks.

2 Heat oil in large baking dish; cook quail, in batches, until browned lightly all over. Drain on absorbent paper.

3 Add garlic, leek and mushrooms to dish; cook, stirring, until leek is soft. Add flour; cook, stirring, 1 minute.

4 Add wine and stock; cook, stirring, until liquid reduces by a half. Stir in puree and sugar.

5 Return quail to dish; cook, covered, in hot oven 30 minutes. Remove cover; cook about 10 minutes or until quail is tender.

6 Serve sprinkled with parsley.

SERVES 6

per serving 38.1g fat; 2619kJ

store Recipe can be made a day ahead and refrigerated, covered.

tucking quail legs into wings

glossary

allspice ground pimento

almonds

BLANCHED skins removed.

GROUND almond meal.

artichoke, globe large flower head of a plant from the thistle family.

bacon rashers bacon slices.

barley a nutritious grain used in soups and stews as well as in whiskey- and beer-making.

bay leaves aromatic leaves from the bay tree.

beans

BORLOTTI (roman beans); pale pink with darker red spots, eaten fresh or dried.

BROAD (fava beans) available fresh, canned or frozen. Fresh are best peeled twice, discarding both the outer long green pod and the sandy-green tough inner shell.

GREEN sometimes called french beans.

HARICOT small, dried white bean similar in appearance and flavour to great northern, navy and canneloni beans.

RED KIDNEY have a floury texture and fairly sweet flavour; colour can vary from pink to maroon.

beef any cuts of beef suitable for stewing are also suitable for casseroles; including blade steak and chuck steak, as listed here, plus gravy beef, rib steak and skirt steak.

BLADE STEAK a cut from the shoulder blade area.

BRISKET from the under section of the forequarter and ribs, rolled and secured with string or netting.

CHUCK STEAK from the neck area; can be used as one piece or as steak.

baby bok choy   bok choy

SPARE RIBS we used the shorter spare ribs which are quite lean but meaty; these are also known as baby back ribs.

belacan (belachan and blachan) dried shrimp paste sold in slabs or flat cakes.

bok choy (pak choi or chinese white cabbage) has a fresh, mild mustard taste and is good braised or in stir-fries. Baby bok choy is also available.

brandy spirit distilled from wine.

breadcrumbs, stale use 1- or 2-day-old bread made into crumbs by grating, blending or processing.

butter use salted or unsalted (sweet) butter; 125g is equal to one stick butter.

cajun seasoning combination of dried ingredients consisting of salt, peppers, garlic, onion and spices.

calamari a type of squid.

capers pickled buds of a Mediterranean shrub.

capsicum (pepper or bell pepper) seeds and membrane should be discarded before use.

caraway seeds a member of the parsley family; available

capers

tiny capers

in seed or ground form and can be used in sweet and savoury dishes.

cardamom native to India and purchased in pod, seed or ground form; has a distinctive aromatic, sweetly rich flavour.

cayenne pepper a thin-fleshed, long, extremely hot red chilli; usually purchased dried and ground.

celeriac tuberous root with brown skin, white flesh and a celery-like flavour.

cheese

BOCCONCINI small balls of mild, delicate cheese packaged in water or whey to keep them white and soft; any yellowing indicates they are old.

PARMESAN sharp-tasting hard cheese used as a flavour accent. We use fresh parmesan cheese, although it is available already finely grated.

chicken

BREAST with skin and bone intact.

BREAST FILLET no skin and bones.

DRUMSTICK leg with skin intact.

LOVELY LEG (drummette) skinless drumstick with the end of the bone removed.

MARYLAND leg and thigh with skin intact.

THIGH has skin and bone intact.

THIGH CUTLET has skin and centre bone intact; sometimes called a chicken chop.

THIGH FILLET no skin and bones.

chickpeas (garbanzos) an irregularly round, sandy coloured legume.

chillies available in many different types and sizes. Use

rubber gloves when chopping fresh chillies as they can burn your skin.

cinnamon stick dried inner bark of the shoots of the cinnamon tree.

coconut

CREAM the first pressing from grated mature coconut flesh.

MILK the second pressing (less rich) from grated mature coconut flesh.

cornflour cornstarch.

corn relish thick spread consisting of corn, celery, onion, capsicum, spices and mustard.

couscous a fine cereal made from semolina.

cream fresh pouring cream; has a minimum fat content of 35 per cent.

SOUR a thick commercially cultured soured cream

THICKENED (whipping) has a minimum fat content of 35 per cent; and includes a thickener.

eggplant aubergine.

english spinach a soft-leafed vegetable, more delicate in taste than silverbeet (swiss chard); young silverbeet can be substituted.

fennel has a slight aniseed taste when fresh, ground or in seed form. The bulb can be eaten uncooked in salads or braised, steamed or stir-fried.

fish sauce made from the liquid drained from salted, fermented anchovies. Has a strong smell and taste; use sparingly. Several varieties are available and the intensity of flavour varies. We used thai fish sauce.

five spice powder a pungent mixture of ground spices including cinnamon, cloves, fennel, star anise and sichuan peppers.

flour, white plain all-purpose flour.

ghee a pure butter fat; it can be heated to high temperatures without burning because of the lack of salts and milk solids.

herbs we have specified when to use fresh or dried herbs. If substituting dried herbs for

broad beans
borlotti beans
red lentils
ckpeas
haricot beans
red kidney beans

english spinach

silverbeet

fresh, use dried (not ground) herbs in the proportions of 1:4, e.g., 1 teaspoon dried herbs instead of 4 teaspoons (1 tablespoon) chopped fresh herbs.

italian sausages large fresh pork sausages, salted lightly.

jalapeno peppers hot chillies, available in brine in bottles and cans.

jam a preserve of sugar and fruit.

juniper berries aromatic flavour; an ingredient of gin.

kumara orange sweet potato.

lamb any cuts of lamb suitable for stewing are also suitable for casseroles.

CHUMP CHOP the chump is the cut from just above the hind legs to the mid-loin section; it can be used as a piece for roasting, or cut into chops.

CUTLET small, tender rib chop.

DICED cubed lean meat.

DRUMSTICKS also known as frenched shanks and trimmed shanks; these are lamb shanks with the gristle that's attached at the lower end removed and the bone trimmed.

LEG from the hindquarter.

NECK CHOP we used 'best' neck chops.

RACK row of cutlets.

ROLLED SHOULDER boneless section of the forequarter, rolled and secured with string or netting.

SHANK forequarter leg.

lard fat obtained from melting down and clarifying pork fat; available packaged.

leek a member of the onion family; resembles the green onion, but is much larger.

lemon grass lemon-tasting, sharp edged grass; The white lower stem is used. Strips of lemon zest can be substituted.

lentils many different varieties of dried legumes; often identified by and named after their colour.

madeira wine fortified with brandy.

mixed spice a blend of ground spices, consisting of cinnamon, allspice and nutmeg.

mushrooms

BUTTON small, cultivated white mushrooms having a delicate, subtle flavour.

FLAT large, soft, flat mushrooms with a rich earthy flavour.

SHIITAKE (chinese black mushrooms) have a unique meaty flavour. Available fresh and dried.

SWISS BROWN light to dark brown mushrooms with full-bodied flavour. Button or cup

mushrooms can be substituted.

mussels should be bought from a fish market, fresh and closed tightly. Before cooking, scrub shells with a strong brush to remove the "beards". Discard any shells that do not open after cooking.

mustard

FRENCH plain mild mustard.

SEEDED (wholegrain) a French-style coarse-grain mustard made from mustard seeds and dijon-style french mustard.

nutmeg the dried nut of an evergreen tree native to Indonesia; also available in ground form.

oil

OLIVE a blend of refined and virgin olive oils, good for everyday cooking.

PEANUT made from ground peanuts, is the most commonly-used oil in Asian cooking; however, a lighter, salad type of oil can be used.

VEGETABLE we used a polyunsaturated vegetable oil.

okra also known as bamia or lady fingers; a green ridged, oblong pod with furry skin.

onion

GREEN (scallion or incorrectly, shallot) an immature onion picked before the bulb has formed, having a long, bright-green edible stalk.

RED large purplish-red onion.

SPRING have crisp, narrow green-leafed tops and a fairly large sweet white bulb.

pancetta cured pork belly; bacon can be substituted.

paprika ground dried red capsicum; available sweet or hot.

parsnip root vegetable shaped like a carrot; has a herb-like flavour.

peanut butter peanuts ground to a paste; available in crunchy and smooth varieties.

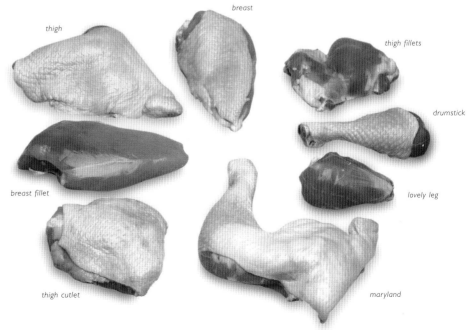

thigh
breast
thigh fillets
drumstick
breast fillet
lovely leg
thigh cutlet
maryland

celeriac

kumara

parsnip

fennel

globe artichoke

pork any cuts of pork suitable for stewing are also suitable for casseroles.

FOREQUARTER CHOPS from the shoulder area.

NECK boneless cut.

port a rich, sweet dessert wine fortified with brandy.

prawns shrimp.

prosciutto uncooked, unsmoked, cured ham; ready to eat when bought.

prunes whole dried plums.

puff pastry, ready-rolled frozen sheets of puff pastry.

rabbit, cutlets rabbit legs.

rice

BASMATI a white, fragrant long-grained rice; should be washed several times before cooking.

JASMINE aromatic long-grain white rice.

LONG-GRAIN elongated grain, remains separate when cooked.

sambal oelek (ulek or olek) a salty paste made from ground chillies.

scallops we used the scallops with coral (roe) attached.

seasoned pepper a combination of black pepper, sugar and bell pepper.

sesame seeds there are two types, black and white; we used the white variety. To toast, spread seeds evenly onto oven tray, toast in moderate oven for about

5 minutes or stir over heat in heavy-based pan until golden brown.

sherry fortified wine consumed as an apertif or used in cooking. Sold as fino (light, dry), amontillado (medium sweet, dark) and oloroso (full-bodied, very dark).

snow peas also known as mange tout (eat all).

soy sauce made from fermented soy beans.

star anise the dried star-shaped fruit of an evergreen tree. It is used sparingly in Chinese cooking and has an aniseed flavour.

stock 1 cup (250ml) stock is equivalent to 1 cup (250ml) water plus 1 crumbled stock cube (or 1 teaspoon crumbled stock powder).

sugar we used coarse granulated table sugar, also known as crystal sugar, unless otherwise specified.

BROWN a soft fine granulated sugar containing molasses.

PALM (gula jawa, gula melaka and jaggery) fine sugar from the coconut palm; sold in cakes. Brown or black sugar can be substituted.

swede a type of turnip; also as rutabaga.

sweet potato fleshy white root vegetable.

tamarind sauce if unavailable, soak about 30g dried tamarind in a cup of hot water, stand 10 minutes, squeeze pulp as dry as possible and use the flavoured water.

tomato

PASTE a concentrated tomato puree used for flavouring.

PUREE canned pureed tomatoes (not tomato paste). Fresh, peeled, pureed tomatoes may be substituted.

SUN-DRIED (de-hydrated tomatoes) we used sun-dried tomatoes packaged in oil, unless otherwise specified.

turmeric a member of the ginger family; its root is dried and ground. It is intensely pungent in taste, but not hot.

veal the meat from a very young calf; identified by its pale pink flesh.

CUTLET choice chop from the mid-loin (back) area.

DICED cubed lean meat.

FOREQUARTER area containing neck, shoulder and ribs.

OSSO BUCCO this famous Italian dish used the hind or forequarter shank or knuckle cut into medallions. When the knuckle is trimmed of meat at the thin end, this is known as a 'Frenched' knuckle.

SHOULDER from the forequarter.

STEAK schnitzel.

vinegar

BALSAMIC originated in the province of Modena, Italy. Regional wine is specially processed then aged in antique wooden casks to give a pungent flavour.

BROWN MALT made from fermented malt and beech shavings.

WHITE made from spirit of cane sugar.

WHITE WINE made from white wine.

worcestershire sauce a thin, dark-brown spicy sauce used as a seasoning for meat, gravies and cocktails and as a condiment.

zucchini courgette.

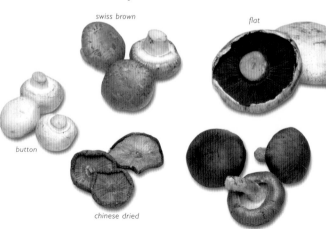

swiss brown

flat

button

chinese dried

shiitake

index

make your own stock

These recipes can be made up to 4 days ahead and stored, covered, in the refrigerator. Be sure to remove any fat from the surface after the cooled stock has been refrigerated overnight. If the stock is to be kept longer, it is best to freeze it in smaller quantities. *All stock recipes make about 2.5 litres (10 cups).*

Stock is also available in cans or tetra packs. Stock cubes or powder can be used. As a guide, 1 teaspoon of stock powder or 1 small crumbled stock cube mixed with 1-cup (250ml) water will give a fairly strong stock. Be aware of the salt and fat content of stock cubes and powders and prepared stocks.

BEEF STOCK

2kg meaty beef bones
2 medium brown onions (300g)
2 untrimmed sticks celery (300g), chopped coarsely
2 medium carrots (250g), chopped coarsely
3 bay leaves
2 teaspoons black peppercorns
5 litres (20 cups) water
3 litres (12 cups) water, extra

Place bones and unpeeled chopped onions in baking dish. Bake in hot oven about 1-hour or until bones and onions are well browned. Transfer bones and onions to large saucepan, add celery, carrots, bay leaves, peppercorns and water, simmer, uncovered, 3 hours. Add extra water, simmer, uncovered, further 1 hour; strain.

CHICKEN STOCK

2kg chicken bones
2 medium brown onions (300g), chopped coarsely
2 untrimmed sticks celery (300g), chopped coarsely
2 medium carrots (250g), chopped coarsely
3 bay leaves
2 teaspoons black peppercorns
5 litres (20 cups) water

Combine ingredients in large saucepan, simmer, uncovered, 2 hours; strain.

FISH STOCK

1.5kg fish bones
3 litres (12 cups) water
1 medium brown onion (150g), chopped coarsely
2 untrimmed sticks celery (300g), chopped coarsely
2 bay leaves
1 teaspoon black peppercorns

Combine ingredients in large saucepan, simmer, uncovered, 20 minutes; strain.

VEGETABLE STOCK

2 large carrots (360g), chopped coarsely
2 large parsnips (360g), chopped coarsley
4 medium brown onions (600g), chopped coarsely
12 untrimmed sticks celery (1.8kg), chopped coarsely
4 bay leaves
2 teaspoons black peppercorns
6 litres (24 cups) water

Combine ingredients in large saucepan, simmer, uncovered, 1¹/2 hours; strain.

conversion chart

MEASURES

One Australian metric measuring cup holds approximately 250ml; one Australian metric tablespoon holds 20ml; one Australian metric teaspoon holds 5ml.

The difference between one country's measuring cups and another's is within a two- or three-teaspoon variance, and will not affect your cooking results. North America, New Zealand and the United Kingdom use a 15ml tablespoon.

All cup and spoon measurements are level. The most accurate way of measuring dry ingredients is to weigh them. When measuring liquids, use a clear glass or plastic jug with the metric markings.

We use large eggs with an average weight of 60g.

DRY MEASURES

METRIC	IMPERIAL
15g	½oz
30g	1oz
60g	2oz
90g	3oz
125g	4oz (¼lb)
155g	5oz
185g	6oz
220g	7oz
250g	8oz (½lb)
280g	9oz
315g	10oz
345g	11oz
375g	12oz (¾lb)
410g	13oz
440g	14oz
470g	15oz
500g	16oz (1lb)
750g	24oz (1½lb)
1kg	32oz (2lb)

LIQUID MEASURES

METRIC	IMPERIAL
30ml	1 fluid oz
60ml	2 fluid oz
100ml	3 fluid oz
125ml	4 fluid oz
150ml	5 fluid oz (¼ pint/1 gill)
190ml	6 fluid oz
250ml	8 fluid oz
300ml	10 fluid oz (½ pint)
500ml	16 fluid oz
600ml	20 fluid oz (1 pint)
1000ml (1 litre)	1¾ pints

LENGTH MEASURES

METRIC	IMPERIAL
3mm	⅛in
6mm	¼in
1cm	½in
2cm	¾in
2.5cm	1in
5cm	2in
6cm	2½in
8cm	3in
10cm	4in
13cm	5in
15cm	6in
18cm	7in
20cm	8in
23cm	9in
25cm	10in
28cm	11in
30cm	12in (1ft)

OVEN TEMPERATURES

These oven temperatures are only a guide for conventional ovens. For fan-forced ovens, check the manufacturer's manual.

	°C (CELSIUS)	°F (FAHRENHEIT)	GAS MARK
Very slow	120	250	½
Slow	150	275-300	1-2
Moderately slow	170	325	3
Moderate	180	350-375	4-5
Moderately hot	200	400	6
Hot	220	425-450	7-8
Very hot	240	475	9

ARE YOU MISSING SOME OF THE WORLD'S FAVOURITE COOKBOOKS?

The Australian Women's Weekly Cookbooks are available from bookshops, cookshops, supermarkets and other stores all over the world. You can also buy direct from the publisher, using the order form below.

TITLE	RRP	QTY	TITLE	RRP	QTY
Asian Meals in Minutes	£6.99		Great Lamb Cookbook	£6.99	
Babies & Toddlers Good Food	£6.99		Greek Cooking Class	£6.99	
Barbecue Meals In Minutes	£6.99		Healthy Heart Cookbook	£6.99	
Basic Cooking Class	£6.99		Indian Cooking Class	£6.99	
Beginners Cooking Class	£6.99		Japanese Cooking Class	£6.99	
Beginners Simple Meals	£6.99		Kids' Birthday Cakes	£6.99	
Beginners Thai	£6.99		Kids Cooking	£6.99	
Best Food	£6.99		Lean Food	£6.99	
Best Food Desserts	£6.99		Low-carb, Low-fat	£6.99	
Best Food Fast	£6.99		Low-fat Feasts	£6.99	
Best Food Mains	£6.99		Low-fat Food For Life	£6.99	
Cakes, Biscuits & Slices	£6.99		Low-fat Meals in Minutes	£6.99	
Cakes Cooking Class	£6.99		Main Course Salads	£6.99	
Caribbean Cooking	£6.99		Middle Eastern Cooking Class	£6.99	
Casseroles	£6.99		Midweek Meals in Minutes	£6.99	
Chicken	£6.99		Muffins, Scones & Breads	£6.99	
Chicken Meals in Minutes	£6.99		New Casseroles	£6.99	
Chinese Cooking Class	£6.99		New Classics	£6.99	
Christmas Cooking	£6.99		New Finger Food	£6.99	
Chocolate	£6.99		Party Food and Drink	£6.99	
Cocktails	£6.99		Pasta Meals in Minutes	£6.99	
Cooking for Friends	£6.99		Potatoes	£6.99	
Creative Cooking on a Budget	£6.99		Salads: Simple, Fast & Fresh	£6.99	
Detox	£6.99		Saucery	£6.99	
Dinner Beef	£6.99		Sauces (May '06)	£6.99	
Dinner Lamb	£6.99		Sensational Stir-Fries	£6.99	
Dinner Seafood	£6.99		Short-order Cook	£6.99	
Easy Australian Style	£6.99		Slim	£6.99	
Easy Curry	£6.99		Sweet Old Fashioned Favourites	£6.99	
Easy Spanish-Style	£6.99		Thai Cooking Class	£6.99	
Essential Soup	£6.99		Vegetarian Meals in Minutes	£6.99	
Freezer, Meals from the	£6.99		Vegie Food	£6.99	
French Food, New	£6.99		Weekend Cook	£6.99	
Fresh Food for Babies & Toddlers	£6.99		Wicked Sweet Indulgences	£6.99	
Get Real, Make a Meal	£6.99		Wok Meals in Minutes	£6.99	
Good Food Fast	£6.99		TOTAL COST:	£	

Mr/Mrs/Ms _____

Address _____

_____ Postcode _____

Day time phone _____ Email* (optional) _____

I enclose my cheque/money order for £ _____

or please charge £ _____

to my: ☐ Access ☐ Mastercard ☐ Visa ☐ Diners Club

PLEASE NOTE: WE DO NOT ACCEPT SWITCH OR ELECTRON CARDS

Card number | | | | | | | | | | | | | | | | |

Expiry date _____ 3 digit security code *(found on reverse of card)* _____

Cardholder's name_____ Signature _____

To order: Mail or fax – photocopy or complete the order form above, and send your credit card details or cheque payable to: Australian Consolidated Press (UK), Moulton Park Business Centre, Red House Road, Moulton Park, Northampton NN3 6AQ, phone (+44) (0) 1604 497531 fax (+44) (0) 1604 497533, e-mail books@acpmedia.co.uk or order online at www.acpuk.com
Non-UK residents: We accept the credit cards listed on the coupon, or cheques, drafts or International Money Orders payable in sterling and drawn on a UK bank. Credit card charges are at the exchange rate current at the time of payment.
Postage and packing UK: Add £1.00 per order plus 50p per book.
Postage and packing overseas: Add £2.00 per order plus £1.00 per book.
All pricing current at time of going to press and subject to change/availability.
Offer ends 31.12.2006

* By including your email address, you consent to receipt of any email regarding this magazine, and other emails which inform you of ACP's other publications, products, services and events, and to promote third party goods and services you may be interested in.